ONE G

MW01136200

MOSES

"I found my mind being stretched and my heart stirred as I read Heather Kendall's *One Greater Than Moses: A History of New Covenant Theology.* Her explanations of a Christ-centered approach to the Bible's storyline helps clarify many issues arising in the thinking of any serious Bible reader. And, her well-documented recounting of God's providence in raising up the New Covenant Theology movement draws in the reader with engaging stories of real people as they wrestled with their own understanding and sometimes with one another in an attempt to be faithful to God's precious Word."

—DR. LARRY E. MCCALL

Pastor, Christ's Covenant Church, Winona Lake, Indiana
Director of Walking Like Jesus Ministries

"Heather Kendall has produced a work that is long overdue and longed for by many that have concerns about the veracity and historicity of NCT. Her careful combing through Church history by interring remnant gems lodged in the writings of many of the early Fathers and Protestant Reformers has lent credence to the more recent exegesis by Christotelic thinkers who birthed this finer hermeneutical approach. Her research has demonstrated to the skeptics of NCT that its teachings are not as novel as they surmised, not as errant as theologians have supposed and not as antinomian as critics have assumed."

—GARY GEORGE

Pastor of Sovereign Grace Chapel, Southbridge, Massachusetts

"Who could have foreseen the influence New Covenant Theology (by whatever name) would come to have in this last generation? It's a story that needed to be told, and all sides of the discussion are indebted to Heather Kendall for telling it for us."

—FRED G. ZASPEL

Pastor, Reformed Baptist Church, Franconia, Pennsylvania, Executive Editor, Books At a Glance, Adjunct Professor of Christian Theology, The Southern Baptist Theological Seminary

"As a Christian historian who is also committed to what has been termed Evangelical Calvinism, I have been fascinated by the clear revival of these biblical truths in the West in the past fifty years or so. This revival, like all such times of renewal, has taken different patterns and shapes. In this extremely helpful narrative, Heather Kendall has recounted the story of one of these patterns, that which has come to be known as New Covenant Theology. The time for recounting this story is surely now, when nearly all of the pioneers of this perspective on the doctrines of grace are still living—though "pioneers" may not be the best word as this theological position has especially tapped into the canonical riches found in the book of Hebrews. Kendall is to be heartily commended for the challenge of writing current history (always difficult as any historian knows) and providing future generations with a clear account of the genesis of this theological pattern. Anyone seriously interested in Reformed theology will be fascinated by this theological story, in which, amazingly Canadians play a leading role!"

—MICHAEL A. G. HAYKIN

Professor of Church History and Biblical Spirituality, Southern Baptist Theological Seminary, Louisville, Kentucky

"Heather Kendall has meticulously researched the inner workings and writings of those who have labored over the past four decades to help provide a more accurate way to interpret the Holy Scriptures. This well documented, readable primer provides a wealth of background information for all those who are coming to understand that New Covenant Theology is all about God's beloved Son. Its clarion message is as old as the sacred New Testament Scriptures. The one greater than Moses is here: His name is Jesus. 'Listen to Him!'"

—GARY D. LONG

Faculty President, Providence Theological Seminary, Franklin, Tennessee

"Writing as an author, Heather Kendall, offers a fundamental background of the early stages of the New Covenant Theology movement in the mid-1900's. She has traced the emphasis on the New Covenant as far back as the early Church Fathers. But her primary work has been on the modern roots and development of the New Covenant Theology in the United States. Kendall's research is remarkable in setting forth the early participants and why they were motivated to challenge traditions in light of 'Sola Scriptura.' I wrote in 1980 concerning the reason for meeting at the Council on Baptist Theology: 'It is convened because we cannot ignore certain urgent issues raised concerning the law and covenants, the relationship between the two testaments, and the standard of ethics. The present crisis calls for immediate action.' Kendall has given a concise, balanced and candid history of New Covenant Theology. May you find this work encouraging and engaging to the point of focusing on 'Christ,' the mediator of the New Covenant.

—RONALD W. MCKINNEY

Pastor, Kinsey Drive Baptist Church, Dalton, Georgia

First Edition

Cover design and layout by Rafael Polendo (polendo.net)
Cover image by GeorgiosArt (photodune.net)

ISBN 978-1-938480-16-4

This volume is printed on acid free paper and meets ANSI Z39.48 standards.

Printed in the United States of America

 QUOIR

Published by Quoir
Orange, California

www.quoir.com

ONE GREATER THAN MOSES

A HISTORY OF
NEW COVENANT THEOLOGY

BY

HEATHER A. KENDALL

THANK YOU FOR THE ENCOURAGEMENT AND/OR
HELPFUL INPUT FROM THE FOLLOWING PEOPLE:

Moe Bergeron, James Clemens, Les Clemens, William Dicks, Roger Fellows, René Frey, Gary George, Douglas Goodin, Michael Haykin, John T. Jeffery, Joe Kelley, Larry E. McCall, Jacob Moseley, Lloyd E. and Judith Scayler, David Sitton, Curtis C. Thomas, Geoff Volker, Joan Wellum, Kirk Wellum, Stephen Wellum, A. Blake White, Ernest Wood, Fred G. Zaspel

SPECIAL THANKS TO:

Gary D. Long, Ronald W. McKinney, John G. Reisinger, and Jon Zens. Thank you also for the helpful insights of my editor, Christa McKirland.

CONTENTS

FOREWORD

I'll never forget my meeting with three brothers in Little Rock, Arkansas, on a Monday in February, 1977. I had spoken in an assembly over the weekend, and they wanted to have a time with me before I drove back to Nashville, Tennessee. They had specific things they wanted to go over with me, and one of them came in the form of a question: "Have you read *The Reformers and Their Stepchildren* by Leonard Verduin?" I told them Walt Hibbard pushed that volume on me when his book venture was operating out of his garage in Maryland, but I had not read it yet. They strongly encouraged me to read it.

In June, 1977, I finally read *Reformers* and it changed my world forever. It put the disconnected pieces of information in my head together in a way that was unbelievably liberating, and my focus on Christ was clarified and accelerated.

It was just months later that I felt compelled to write about the issues raised in *Reformers*, and other related concerns. As a result, "Is There A 'Covenant of Grace'?" appeared in the Autumn, 1977, issue of *Baptist Reformation Review*.

This article caused quite a stir, and John Reisinger called it "the first shot fired in twenty years" at a gathering in Dalton, Georgia. Thus began a journey of many to develop, discuss, and unpack the implications of the centrality of Christ in the New Covenant.

Heather Kendall has accomplished a great service to the body of Christ by compiling her historical study of the blossoming of "New Covenant Theology" at the end of the 20th Century. She has painstakingly researched the subject and pieced together a fair, balanced and engaging presentation of an important segment of history.

I know you will be uplifted and challenged by Heather's contemporary history of how Christ's pre-eminence came to the fore once again, and her drawing together of quotations from the past showing that the finality of the New Covenant was recognized by many others. *One Greater than Moses* is an important contribution to the ongoing work of Christ on earth.

— JON ZENS

Author of "'This Is My Beloved Son, Hear Him': The Foundation for New Covenant Ethics and Ecclesiology," and editor of *Searching Together* since 1978.

INTRODUCTION

Many believers consider New Covenant Theology (NCT) a new phenomenon or even a passing fancy. Because so many do not know the modern development of this movement, I want to leave a written record for posterity. All humans, including believers, tend to cling to the familiar. In addition, we tend toward ignorance of our own history and the history of our beliefs.

Therefore I admire those men in the mid to late 1900s who questioned teachings in their respective churches in an effort to remain faithful to the Scriptures. Please understand I am writing about men who confronted fellow believers who had differing ideas of what the Bible teaches. I hope by the end of this history that readers will express sympathy and appreciation for Jon Zens, John Reisinger, Ron McKinney and Gary Long. Those men challenged their friends and relatives with God's Word. The significance of these men breaking with tradition should not escape our notice as it involved a slow step by step process. Breaking with tradition was not instantaneous.

New Covenant Theology explains how the Old and New Testaments fit together—the big picture in the Bible. Before beginning this history, I need to assume three important facts for myself and my readers.

First, sinners may have their sins forgiven and be reconciled to God—only through the shed blood of Christ on Calvary. When Jesus died on the cross, he paid the penalty that we deserved to receive for our rebellion against God. When Jesus rose from the grave, God the Father accepted his sacrifice once and forever. Whoever genuinely repents of sin, turns in faith to God, and accepts Christ's sacrifice as satisfying the wrath of God for his or her sins will live forever with God in the new heavens and new earth.

Second, repentance and faith require an act of will. For this reason, the church of Christ consists only of believers. Each one must answer to God for his or her own sin. No one else may do this for another person. Nevertheless the Holy Spirit must first open the spiritual eyes of sinners to their need for the Savior.

Finally, the Holy Spirit dwells within a believer and enables that person to persevere to the end. Sanctification or growing in the knowledge of God and becoming more like Jesus continues as a life-long undertaking. Since all believers participate in this process of sanctification, we must first examine our own hearts. Before trying to correct another person's beliefs, we must ask ourselves these questions: Do I exhibit a teachable spirit? Does the other person's belief downgrade the supremacy of God or of the Lord Jesus? Does their belief change or affect the doctrine of salvation? Finally, how does their belief affect their view of the blood sacrifice of Jesus?

Since the Holy Spirit is always teaching all true believers, we must be careful how we treat our brothers and sisters in the faith. We must also make sure that we are on solid ground biblically before correcting another believer. If their teaching weakens the Gospel or downgrades the supremacy of Jesus, then we must present the Word in truth and with gentleness.

After carefully studying Scripture, author and theologian, Jon Zens, felt compelled to write an article questioning the covenant of grace in covenant theology. The storyline of this theology flat lines Scripture and allows for the transfer of ideas back and forth between the old covenant era and the new covenant era. As a result the nation of Israel becomes a model for the church. The Ten Commandments become the means of convicting sinners of their need for a Savior and afterward the rule of law for the believer. (I shall explain covenant theology in more detail in chapter one.) In contrast, Zens believed a Christocentric reading of the Scriptures would both inform and transform how each believer lives his or her life. The issue for him was the superiority of Jesus over Moses. By insisting that the Ten Commandments are the only rule of law for the believer, covenant theology teaches that Moses has greater authority than Christ.

In December 1978, Don Garlington and Jon Zens had a meeting at the Marriott Hotel in Saddle Brook, New Jersey. As a covenant theologian, Don had written a challenge to Jon's article. In the course of their conversation, Jon asked Don:

> As you know, Puritan Samuel Bolton said in the 1600s, it is a "hard lesson to live above the law, yet walk according to the law; to walk in the law in respect of duty, but to live above it in respect of comfort." Don, do you believe these sentiments are in line with the New Testament revelation?
>
> NCT answers this question with a resolute, "No." And out of such considerations NCT feels strongly that the old covenant order is over, and that a new covenant—and a new and living way—has been inaugurated by Jesus Christ. NCT is concerned to open up the big picture, to see all of history moving toward the incarnation of the Son of God.[1]

Let me reiterate. This history will be talking about believers disagreeing with believers—friends and brothers on opposite

---

1   Jon Zens, e-mail message, March 2015.

sides. Peer pressure often prevents people from admitting they have made a mistake. I pray this history will be sensitive to feelings but will stand for the truth.

CHAPTER I

WHY NEW COVENANT THEOLOGY?

Understanding the big picture in the Bible should be one of the first steps for a believer after salvation. Nevertheless theologians have been arguing about the biblical storyline for almost 500 years.[1] Until recently evangelicals have taught two different storylines for Scripture: covenant theology and dispensationalism. Neither considered the existence of a third way of putting the Old and New Testaments together.

COVENANT THEOLOGY

The roots of covenant theology go back to the beginning of time. Since the formation of city-states, government and religion have joined together. Christian Roman emperors continued the practice. Having been raised a devout Catholic, Martin Luther firmly believed in the union of Church and State. When he nailed his Ninety-five Theses to the Wittenberg Church door on October 31, 1517, he changed the world forever. It was the birth of Protestantism. Although Luther preached salvation by faith alone, he never changed his attitude toward the union of Church and State. Other Reformers maintained the same position. Thus

---

1.   The 16th century Anabaptists challenged the storyline of the Reformers, as we shall see in chapter 3.

the coalition of government and religion continued in Protestant countries as well as in Catholic ones.[2]

Eventually Johann Cocceius (1603–1669), a professor in Franeker and Leyden, built on the teaching of Zwingli (1484–1531) and developed the storyline called covenant theology, consisting of three main covenants. Before the world existed, the Triune God made a covenant of redemption. The Father purposed salvation; the Son purchased salvation; and the Holy Spirit applies salvation. Then God gave Adam a covenant of works. But he disobeyed God by eating the fruit from the tree of knowledge of good and evil. As the representative head of all humanity, Adam's sin became our sin. This means everyone must suffer the consequence of Adam's sin. We are born sinners with a natural inclination to sin. After the failure of the covenant of works, God promised a covenant of grace through Jesus Christ. Thus all the covenants in the Bible fall under the one overarching covenant of grace.

The old covenant and the new covenant are two administrations or dispensations of the covenant of grace. Therefore these theologians transferred the principles of God's rule over the nation of Israel to the church—the union of religion and state, the right for the state to punish those who break God's laws, the transfer of the rite of circumcision to the practice of infant baptism. The theonomists of today consistently believe in following those three principles. Most reformed believers, however, only insist on infant baptism for all babies born to church members.

---

2. Heather A. Kendall, "The Bible's Storyline: How It Affects the Doctrine of Salvation," *Journal for Baptist Theology & Ministry*, 8, no. 1 (Spring 2011): 62, last modified (Spring 2011), accessed January 28, 2015, http://baptistcenter.net/journals/JBTM_8-1_Spring_2011.pdf#page=62.

Covenant theologians divide the Law given to Moses into moral, civil and ceremonial commands. Only the nation of Israel must obey all the civil and ceremonial laws. But the moral law is God's unchanging eternal law. Therefore it applies to us today. Since the Ten Commandments are the unchanging moral law of God, even Christ cannot change or add to them. Thus Christians remain under Moses' authority. The result of this teaching is that Moses has more authority than Christ.

DISPENSATIONALISM

The second storyline to consider is dispensationalism. It is an offshoot of premillennialism whose roots go back to the years between the Old and New Testaments. The *Pseudepigrapha* is a collection of writings by Jewish authors between 200 BC and AD 100. We may trace the development of premillennialism through those writings. Every author assumed the name of a famous person from the past and wrote in response to current events. Since premillennialism only describes the end of God's story, it is not a biblical storyline in and of itself. Dispensationalism, however, does attempt to explain the storyline of the Bible.

After apostolic times historic premillennialists became preoccupied with determining the date of Jesus' return. They longed for Jesus to come and establish his kingdom on earth. This hope was not surprising. To state churches, these believers were heretics. As such, state churches often persecuted them.

In the early 1800s, as an aftermath of the French Revolution, the prophetic parts of the Bible began to fascinate many people in England. Those believers thought that the Bible explained the course of future events, and they believed that they were living in those times. Prophetic conferences became popular. Lady Powerscourt held such a conference, controlled mainly by the

Plymouth Brethren, annually from 1831 to 1833. J. N. Darby attended her conference near Dublin in 1833. F. Roy Coad explains, "Darby threw himself wholeheartedly into this fervour of prophetic expectation and discussion."[3]

After this Darby travelled extensively teaching the rapture of the church before the coming of Antichrist. Eschatology became central to the message of the Plymouth Brethren. Preachers would teach the urgency of repentance and faith in Jesus before it was too late. Because of Darby's passion for eschatology and willingness to travel to foreign countries, many people believe in dispensational theology today.

Dispensationalists trace two biblical storylines. God has one plan for Israel and another for the church. The plan for Israel involves an earthly political kingdom, whereas the church looks forward to a heavenly spiritual kingdom. Thus Israel and the church are mutually exclusive. Classical dispensationalism teaches that the church is an afterthought in the divine plan because the Jews rejected Jesus. Progressive dispensationalists no longer believe that idea. Instead those theologians understand that God always intended to redeem the church through the death, resurrection and exultation of Christ. But God still plans to fulfill his land promise to Abraham in a future millennium on this present earth. Not many believe classical dispensationalism today. Most dispensationalists are progressive.

NEW COVENANT THEOLOGY

New covenant theologians believe in a Christ-centered story-line and the unity of the Scriptures. They believe the Bible to be one long upward progressive storyline from the fall of man

---

3. F. Roy Coad, *History of the Brethren Movement* (Grand Rapids, MI: Eerdmans, 1968), 109.

to the consummation in the new heavens and new earth. The backbone of this storyline is the covenantal nature of God as he accomplishes his plans through his covenants with people. "I will be your God and you will be my people." The focal point of God's story culminates in Jesus Christ. All humans fail by becoming covenant breakers. In contrast, Christ fulfills God's plan to create an eternal covenant-keeping people.

Since there are 400 years between the Old and New Testaments, scholars have divided the Bible into those two sections. By doing this, we have a clue of what a Christ-centered storyline means. The Old Testament relates how God prepared for the coming of his Son while the New Testament tells his story from the birth of Christ to the end of time. Thus Jesus remains the central character in God's story.

Before time began, God planned to form a community of redeemed people who would worship and praise him forever. As soon as Adam and Eve rebelled against God and sinned, God promised to send the Savior, the promised Seed. The Old Testament gradually reveals more of Jesus, who is this promised Seed. Since Israel was an important building block in God's plan, he set the Israelites apart to be his special people. Therefore the Mosaic covenant is like the foundation of a house. God gradually revealed more of his plan of salvation to Israel and prepared a family for Jesus to be born into.

The New Testament represents the house built upon the foundation of the Old Testament. It tells God's story during the New Covenant era, this present age in which God is building his eternal kingdom, the church, consisting of Jew and Gentile. The climax of the biblical story occurs at Jesus' death, resurrection and exaltation as King. At Jesus' return, the following events will occur: the general resurrection of the dead, the destruction of this present earth by fire and the general judgment. God will consign non-believers to hell and gather the redeemed to live forever with him in the new heavens and new earth.

The central issue for new covenant theology concerns the grammatical-historical approach of redemptive history. Nevertheless during the course of its development two other pillars of the faith developed: a believers-only church and the doctrines of grace. I shall delve into the history and meaning of both of those beliefs later in the book.

A CRITIQUE OF THE THREE VIEWS

New covenant theologians do agree in part with some teachings in covenant theology and dispensationalism. But a proper view of Jesus Christ and his work on the cross is at stake. Stephen Wellum, a professor of systematic theology, pinpoints the weaknesses of covenant theology and dispensationalism. Both base their storyline firmly on the unconditional covenant with Abraham. For covenant theology, the genealogical principle— "to you and your children"—remains constant across redemptive history. For dispensationalism, the land promise remains unchanging for the nation of Israel.[4]

In the New Testament, the church consists only of believers whereas covenant theology encourages a mixed multitude of believers and non-believers as members of the church. This means that some people may have a false security of their salvation. Also, because of the overarching covenant of grace, covenant theologians insist that Moses has more authority over the believer than Christ. But believers are not under the command of Moses; rather they are under Christ's authority. This means

4. Stephen J. Wellum, in Peter J. Gentry and Stephen J. Wellum, *Kingdom through Covenant* (Wheaton, IL: Crossway, 2012), 117, 118.

that Christ has the right to interpret Moses' Law for new covenant believers. Nevertheless new covenant believers do walk in the same way of righteousness and holiness as God commanded the Israelites. But we must interpret the principles found in Moses' Law from a new covenant perspective.

In the case of dispensationalism, the idea of a restored Jewish temple with priests who perform animal sacrifices insults Jesus' precious blood. In addition, most of the Israelites in the nation of Israel did not have the right heart attitude toward God. Much of what they did was outward ritual. Therefore those people have forfeited their right to be part of God's kingdom of redeemed believers. The New Testament is clear that God has broken down the wall of partition between the Jew and Gentile. Thus Abraham's spiritual seed consists of the believing remnant of Israelites in the Old Testament and the believing Jews and Gentiles united in the church by faith in Christ. As Gentiles, we should be thankful for the believing Jews who spread the Gospel throughout the world. This means that the land promise will come true on the new heavens and new earth for the church, including the redeemed in the nation of Israel.

Today believers live in the day of grace, not under the legalism of Judaism. Because the Old Testament prophets waited expectantly for Christ, non-believing Jews persecuted them. Once Jesus died and rose again, Judaism became obsolete. True, God ordained Judaism in the Old Testament. But now that Christ has come, Judaism has served its purpose in history. New covenant theologians, however, do need to guard against the dangers of Marcionism—ignoring the Old Testament. We desire to exalt Christ as our King and Savior but not at the expense of dismissing a good part of the Bible. God never changes.

NEW COVENANT THEOLOGY PRESUPPOSITIONS

After studying the history of this movement, I believe new covenant theologians hold certain non-negotiable presuppositions:

- The Scriptures are the inspired, infallible, authoritative Word of God. Their purpose is to bring glory to the Triune God by revealing who Jesus is: the Son of God and the Lord and Savior of a redeemed people, the church. "All Scripture is God-breathed and is useful for teaching, rebuking, correcting and training in righteousness" (2 Tim. 3:16, NIV).

- The Holy Spirit is the author of the Scriptures: "The discernment of the Holy Spirit is absolutely essential for accurately handling the Word of God because *there is no authentic leading of the Holy Spirit that is not contextually wedded to the words of the Bible*" (italics Long's).[5]

- Jesus Christ is the final revelation of God (Luke 9:35; Hebrews 1:1).

- There is only one gospel: God has decisively acted on behalf of sinful men in the person and work of Jesus Christ.[6] All have sinned and rebelled against a holy God. Therefore we deserve to be punished. When Jesus died, was buried, and rose again, he took the punishment of rebellious sinners. God declares all those righteous and forgiven who have repented of their sin and, by faith, have accepted God's gift of salvation through the shed blood of Christ on the cross.

---

5. Gary D. Long, "New Covenant Theology," 1, last modified (2013), accessed November 2, 2015, http://www.ptsco.org/NCT Brochoure Text 2013.pdf.

6. Jon Zens, "After Ten Years: Observations and Burdens On My Heart," *Baptist Reformation Review*, 11, no. 1 (Spring 1982): 24.

- The doctrines of grace: Some are wondering what NCT is all about without realizing that a belief in God's sovereign grace is a fundamental tenet. Such people may not believe that the Scriptures teach both God's sovereignty in salvation and human responsibility. As believers, we cannot understand this tension in Scripture, but we must accept God's Word. It is wrong to make those two truths mutually exclusive or to act as if one of them does not exist. This means that a sovereign grace preacher can honestly plead with his audience to admit that they are sinners, repent and trust in the finished work of Christ on the cross.

- The church of Christ consists only of believers. In the rest of this book, I shall use the expression "believers-only church." By this I mean that the church, or body of Christ, consists only of baptized believers. I do not mean that a non-believer cannot enter the doors of a church building. "How shall they hear without a preacher?" (Romans 10:14, KJV). But the main purpose of the church gathering together should be to worship and adore our Triune God, to give thanks for the sacrifice of Jesus on the cross, and to grow spiritually in Christ.

CHAPTER 2

GLIMPSES OF NEW COVENANT THEOLOGY DEVELOPING BEFORE THE REFORMATION[1]

The current controversy concerns differing opinions on the relation between the Old and New Testaments. Covenant theologians flat line the two testaments and put Moses, or the old covenant, on an equal footing with Christ, or the new covenant. Then they allow the transfer of ideas between the two testaments or dispensations. One such transfer results in the Ten Commandments having more authority over believers than Christ. Dispensationalists build a wedge between the Testaments and separate Israel from the church. New covenant theologians teach the grammatical-historical approach of redemptive history and the centrality of Christ.[2] While a seminary student, A. Blake White wrote a paper—later published as a book. In it he states, "More than any other system, New Covenant Theology does justice to the progressive nature of Scripture by seeking to let biblical theology inform systematic

---

1 For further glimpses of NCT developing before the Reformation see the Appendix.

2 Gary D. Long, *Context! Evangelical Views On The Millennium Examined*, 3rd ed. (Charleston, SC: www.CreateSpace.com, 2011), 295, 296.

theology." [3] If NCT is the correct way to interpret the Bible, then we should find glimpses of it developing in early church history.

BARNABAS OF ALEXANDRIA, AD 70–100[4]

Barnabas teaches that God requires people to worship him and to love their neighbor. Barnabas calls this the new law of Christ. For this reason Jewish sacrifices are abolished.

Epistle of Barnabas: Chapter 2 — The Jewish Sacrifices Are Now Abolished

> Since, therefore, the days are evil, and Satan possesses the power of this world, we ought to give heed to ourselves, and diligently inquire into the ordinances of the Lord. Fear and patience, then, are helpers of our faith; and long-suffering and continence are things which fight on our side. While these remain pure in what respects the Lord, Wisdom, Understanding, Science, and Knowledge rejoice along with them. For He hath revealed to us by all the prophets that He needs neither sacrifices, nor burnt-offerings, nor oblations, saying thus, "What is the multitude of your sacrifices unto Me, saith the Lord? I am full of burnt-offerings, and desire not the fat of lambs, and the blood of bulls and goats, not when ye come to appear before Me: for who hath required these things at your hands? Tread no more My courts, not though ye bring with you fine flour. Incense is a vain abomination unto Me, and your new moons and sabbaths I cannot endure." He has therefore abolished these things, that the new law of our Lord Jesus Christ, which is without the yoke of necessity, might have a human oblation. And again He says to them, "Did I command your fathers, when they went out from the land of Egypt, to offer unto Me burnt-offerings and sacrifices? But this rather I commanded them, Let no one of you cherish any evil in his heart against his neighbour, and love

---

3 A. Blake White, *The Newness of the New Covenant* (Frederick, MD: New Covenant Media, 2008), 57.

4 James Orr, *The History and Literature of The Early Church* (London: Hodder and Stoughton, 1913), 56.

not an oath of falsehood." We ought therefore, being possessed of understanding, to perceive the gracious intention of our Father; for He speaks to us, desirous that we, not going astray like them, should ask how we may approach Him. To us, then, He declares, "A sacrifice [pleasing] to God is a broken spirit; a smell of sweet savour to the Lord is a heart that glorifieth Him that made it." We ought therefore, brethren, carefully to inquire concerning our salvation, lest the wicked one, having made his entrance by deceit, should huff us forth from our [true] life.[5]

JUSTIN MARTYR, AD 100–165

Justin Martyr differentiates between the old covenant given by Moses and the new covenant given through Christ. He also teaches that believers are the true spiritual Israel.[6]

Dialogue with Trypho: Chapter 11

"Trypho," I began, "there never will be, nor has there ever been from eternity, any other God except Him who created and formed this universe. Furthermore, we do not claim that our God is different from yours, for He is the God who, with a strong hand and outstretched arm, led your forefathers out of the land of Egypt. Nor have we placed our trust in any other (for, indeed, there is no other), but only in Him whom you also have trusted, the God of Abraham and of Isaac and of Jacob. But, our hope is not through Moses or through the Law, otherwise our customs would be the same as yours. [2] Now, indeed, for I have read, Trypho, that there should be a definitive law and a covenant, more binding than all others, which now must be respected by all those who aspire to the heritage of God. The law promulgated at Horeb is already obsolete, and was intended for you Jews only, whereas the law of which I speak is simply for all men. Now, a

---

5   Barnabas of Alexandria, *Epistle of Barnabas*, chapter 2, last modified (date), accessed September 26, 2014, http://earlychristianwritings.com/text/barnabas-roberts.html.

6   It is more accurate to say that believers belong to the spiritual seed of Abraham.

later law in opposition to an older law abrogates the older; so, too, does a later covenant void an earlier one. An everlasting and final law, Christ Himself, and a trustworthy covenant has been given to us, after which there will be no law, or commandment, or precept. [3] Have you not read these words of Isaiah: *'Give ear to me, and listen to me, my people; and you kings, give ear unto me: for a law will go forth from me, and my judgment will be a light to the nations. My Just One approaches swiftly, and my Savior will go forth, and nations will trust in my arm'* [Isa 51.4-5]? Concerning this New Covenant, God thus spoke through Jeremiah: *'Behold the days will come, says the Lord, and I will make a new covenant with the house of Israel, and with the house of Judah: not according to the covenant which I made with their fathers, in the day that I took them by the hand to bring them out of the land of Egypt'* [Jer 31.31-32]. [4] If, therefore, God predicted that He would make a new covenant, and this for a light to the nations, and we see and are convinced that, through the name of the crucified Jesus Christ, men have turned to God, leaving behind them idolatry and other sinful practices, and have kept the faith and have practiced piety even unto death, then everyone can clearly see from these deeds and the accompanying powerful miracles that He is indeed the New Law, the new covenant, and the expectation of those who, from every nation, have awaited the blessings of God. [5] We have been led to God through this crucified Christ, and we are the true spiritual Israel, and the descendants of Judah, Jacob, Isaac, and Abraham, who, though uncircumcised, was approved and blessed by God because of his faith and was called the father of many nations. All this will be proved as we proceed with our discussion" (italics Edgecomb's).[7]

IRENAEUS, BISHOP OF LYONS, C AD 130–200

Jesus Christ designed both the old and new covenants. Nevertheless the new covenant is superior to the old because in it believers have liberty. The new covenant frees us from bondage

---

7   Justin Martyr, *Dialogue with Trypho*, chapter 11, last modified (date), accessed March 24, 2014, http://www.bombaxo.com/trypho.html.

to sin and from condemnation by the Law. Moreover Irenaeus implies that Abraham looked forward to the liberty and blessings of the new covenant prophesied by Jeremiah.

Against Heresies, 4.9.1

Now, without contradiction, He means by those things which are brought forth from the treasure new and old, the two covenants; the old, that giving of the law which took place formerly; and He points out as the new, that manner of life required by the Gospel, of which David says, "Sing unto the Lord a new song;" and Esaias, "Sing unto the Lord a new hymn. ..." And Jeremiah says: "Behold, I will make a new covenant, not as I made with your fathers" in Mount Horeb. But one and the same householder produced both covenants, the Word of God, our Lord Jesus Christ, who spake with both Abraham and Moses, and who has restored us anew to liberty, and has multiplied that grace which is from Himself.[8]

ORIGEN, C AD 185–254

Gentiles did not have the same privileges as the Israelites whom God had chosen as his special people. As a result the Gentiles had no knowledge of the covenants of God given by Moses or by Jesus.

Contra Celsum – Book 8, Chap. V.

Whilst there are thus many gods and lords, whereof some are such in reality, and others are such only in name, we strive to rise not only above those whom the nations of the earth worship as gods, but also beyond those spoken of as gods in Scripture, of whom they are wholly ignorant who are strangers to the covenants of God given by Moses and by our Saviour Jesus, and

---

8   Irenaeus, *Against Heresies*, 4.9.1, last modified (date), accessed January 7, 2015, http://www.earlychristianwritings.com/text/irenaeus-book4.html.

who have no part in the promises which He has made to us through them.[9]

Tom Wells comments on this passage:

> Origen (c. 185-c. 254) alludes to Ephesians 2:12 which speaks of those who were "excluded from the citizenship in Israel and foreigners to the covenants of promise." He describes these people as "strangers to the covenants of God given by Moses and by our Savior Jesus, and who have no part in the promises which He has made through them." In saying this, he seems to limit the covenants referred to in the Ephesians verse to two, the Mosaic and the New Covenants.[10]

JOHN CHRYSOSTOM, AD 347–407

Chrysostom teaches that the Mosaic Law was a temporary baby-sitter until Christ should come. Faith comes through Christ, not the Law.

Commentary on Galatians 3

> Gal. 3:25, 26. "But now that faith is come which leads to perfect manhood we are no longer under a tutor. For ye are all sons of God through faith in Christ Jesus."

> The Law then, as it was our tutor, and we were kept shut up under it, is not the adversary but the fellow-worker of grace; but if when grace is come, it continues to hold us down, it becomes an adversary; for if it confines those who ought to go forward to grace, then it is the destruction of our salvation. If a candle which gave light by night, kept us, when it became day, from the sun, it would not only not benefit, it would injure us; and so doth the Law, if it stands between us and greater

---

9   Origen, *Contra Celsum,* 8.5, last modified (date), accessed May 28, 2014, http://www.gnosis.org/library/orig_cc8.htm.

10 Tom Wells, "The Christian Appeal of a New Covenant Theology," in Tom Wells and Fred Zaspel, *New Covenant Theology* (Frederick, MD: New Covenant Media, 2002), 25.

benefits. Those then are the greatest traducers of the Law, who still keep it, just as the tutor makes a youth ridiculous, by retaining him with himself, when time calls for his departure. Hence Paul says, "But after faith is come, we are no longer under a tutor." We are then no longer under a tutor, "for ye are all sons of God." Wonderful! see how mighty is the power of Faith, and how he unfolds as he proceeds! Before, he showed that it made them sons of the Patriarch, "Know therefore," says he, "that they which be of faith, the same are sons of Abraham;" now he proves that they are sons of God also, "For ye are all," says he, "sons of God through faith, which is in Christ Jesus;" by Faith, not by the Law. Then, when he has said this great and wonderful thing, he names also the mode of their adoption,

Ver. 27. "For as many of you as were baptized into Christ, did put on Christ."[11]

AUGUSTINE, AD 354–430

Augustine taught that Abraham had three kinds of seeds: physical children who are not the children of promise, physical children who are the children of promise, children of promise who are not Abraham's physical seed.

Epistolae CXCVI, ii, 8; iii, 10, 11; iv, 14.

Let us therefore be Jews of this sort, not of the flesh but of the spirit, as being of the seed of Abraham, not according to the flesh, as are those who with carnal pride glory in bearing his name, but according to the spirit of faith, which these are not,… "For you are all," says the Apostle, "one in Christ Jesus. And if you be Christ's, then you are the seed of Abraham, heirs according to the promise" (Gal 3:28).

According to this interpretation of the Apostle those Jews who are not Christians are not the children of Abraham, although

---

11 Chrysostom, *Commentary on Galatians 3*, last modified (date), accessed May 28, 2014, http://sacred-texts.com/chr/ecf/113/1130008/htm.

according to the flesh they be descended from him. For when he says "Know ye therefore, that they who are of the faith, the same are the children of Abraham", (Gal 3:7) he assuredly means that those who are not of the faith are not children of Abraham... Is it not a most marvellous thing and a profound mystery that there should be many born of Israel who are not Israelites and many who are not children of Abraham though they be of his seed? How is it that they are not his children and that we are, unless it be that they are not "the children of the promise" pertaining to the grace of Christ, but "children of the flesh" bearing a meaningless name? This is why they are not Israelites as we are, for we are Israelites by regeneration according to the spirit, they by generation according to the flesh.[12]

---

12 Augustine, *An Augustine Synthesis,* arranged by Erich Przywara (New York, NY: Harper & Brothers, 1958), 317–318.

CHAPTER 3

GLIMPSES OF NEW COVENANT THEOLOGY DEVELOPING AFTER THE REFORMATION

New covenant theology grew out of the beliefs of two unrelated groups of believers: the Anabaptists in Switzerland and the first generation Particular Baptists in England. The Anabaptists gave us the legacy of the Christ-centered biblical storyline, central to new covenant theology. In addition, they believed the New Testament taught the concept of a believers-only church. The Reformers martyred them because a believers-only church meant the separation of Church and State.

One hundred years later, the first-generation Particular Baptists combined the beliefs of the Anabaptists with Calvin's teaching on the doctrines of grace.[1] Those three tenets—the Christ-centered biblical storyline, the believers-only church, and the doctrines of grace— became the pillars of new covenant theology. After considering the Particular Baptists, I shall discuss

---

1   The doctrines of grace: total depravity, unconditional election, limited atonement, irresistible grace, and perseverance of the saints. I shall explain the doctrines of grace more fully in chapter 4.

some English preachers displaying glimpses of a developing NCT in the 17th and 18th centuries.

THE ANABAPTISTS

The Anabaptist movement began in Switzerland on January 21, 1525, when approximately twelve men rejected the Reformers' insistence on the union of Church and State and a belief in infant baptism. They believed the church should consist only of those saved by the regenerating power of the Holy Spirit. Convinced that church members should be believers, they insisted on believer's baptism and proceeded to baptize each other.[2] Baptism symbolized the public declaration of a repentant heart and a commitment to follow Jesus. From that time on, Anabaptist Churches flourished as more and more believers publicly took a stand through the waters of baptism. William R. Estep, a professor of Church History, writes:

> After his baptism at the hands of Grebel, Blaurock proceeded to baptize all the others present. The newly baptized then pledged themselves as true disciples of Christ to live lives separated from the world and to teach the gospel and hold the faith.
>
> Anabaptism was born. With this first baptism, the earliest church of the Swiss Brethren was constituted. This was clearly the most revolutionary act of the Reformation. No other event so completely symbolized the break with Rome. Here, for the first time in the course of the Reformation, a group of Christians dared to form a church after what was conceived to be the New Testament pattern. The Brethren emphasized the absolute necessity of a personal commitment to Christ as essential to salvation and a prerequisite to baptism.[3]

---

2 William R. Estep, *The Anabaptist Story*, rev. ed. (Grand Rapids, MI: Eerdmans, 1975), 10–11.

3 Ibid., 11.

In 1528 Pilgram Marpeck of Austria joined the Anabaptists. In his writings we discover the clearest glimpse of a Christocentric storyline so far. As Estep explains:

> Marpeck's most creative contribution to Anabaptist thought was his view of the Scriptures. While holding the Scriptures to be the Word of God, he made a distinction between the purpose of the Old Testament and that of the New. As the foundation must be distinguished from the house, the Old Testament must be distinguished from the New. The New Testament was centered in Jesus Christ and alone was authoritative for the Brethren. To hold that the Old Testament was equally authoritative for the Christian was to abolish the distinction between the two.[4]

Furthermore Marpeck taught that God prepared for the coming of Christ in the Old Testament. Therefore God never intended for the Old Testament to be permanent, but a temporary step in his plan to redeem a people for himself. Other Anabaptist writers agreed with him and emphasized the progressive nature of biblical history. Estep continues:

> He [Marpeck] drew some graphic contrasts which emphasize the transitory (*zeitlich*) nature of the Old Testament when compared to the eternal (*ewig*) nature of the New. In the Old Testament there is symbol (*Figur*); in the New the essence (*Wesen*) of that which is symbolized. The Old Testament speaks of Adam, sin, death, and the law; the New Testament centers in the message of redemption through the risen Christ. He alone brings us to the new birth through the power of the Holy Spirit....
>
> Even though there are differing emphases among the various Anabaptist writers in regard to the Scriptures and their use, there are significant areas of agreement. For all Anabaptists the Bible was the only rule of faith and practice for discipleship and the church. Biblical revelation was held to be progressive. The Old Testament was preparatory and partial, whereas the New

---

4   Ibid., 86.

Testament was final and complete. All of the Scriptures, they insisted, must be interpreted Christologically, that is, through the mind of Christ. The Holy Spirit alone can illuminate the letter of the Bible and give it convincing power in the life of the seeker. The Bible is the Word of God, that is, the written Word which brings us to the living Word, who alone can give us new life in the power of the Spirit.[5]

Living about AD 139, Marcion rejected the God of the Old Testament, denied the incarnation of Christ, and deleted all biblical passages in which Jesus claimed the God of the Old Testament as his Father.[6] The Anabaptists did not fall prey to the errors of Marcion. Zachary S. Maxcey quotes a later version of Estep's book for a seminary paper:

> Although they did not reject the Old Testament in a Marcionite fashion, *it was never allowed to take precedence over the New Testament or to become normative for the Christian faith.* Theirs was a New Testament hermeneutic that assumed a progression in a biblical revelation that culminated in the Christ-event. *Therefore the Old Testament, although useful and often quoted, could never stand alone, unqualified by the New Testament* (emphasis Maxcey's).[7]

PARTICULAR BAPTISTS

Over 100 years later, some Particular Baptists in England embraced the same redemptive-historical storyline and the same desire for believer's baptism as the Anabaptists. They seceded from

---

5   Ibid., 142–144.

6   Williston Walker, *A History of the Christian Church*, 3rd ed., revised by Robert T. Handy (New York, NY: Charles Scribner's, 1970), 54, 55.

7   William R. Estep, *The Anabaptist Story: An Introduction to Sixteenth-Century Anabaptism*, 3rd ed. (Grand Rapids, MI: Eerdmans, 1995), 22; cited by Zachary S. Maxcey, "Historical Forerunners of New Covenant Theology," Part 1 of 3, *Providence Theological Seminary Journal*, no. 1 (Nov 2014): 6.

a congregational church in England sometime between 1633 and 1638.[8] Believing in the doctrines of grace, these Baptists remained reformed but rejected the union of Church and State. They separated over a belief in believer's baptism and formed churches consisting only of believers. By 1641, these Baptists practiced believer's baptism by immersion;[9] for they understood baptism to symbolize the death, burial and resurrection of Jesus.

Since England was embroiled in civil war (1642—1649), Particular Baptists had religious freedom to draft The London Baptist Confession of Faith in 1644. They entitled it, "The Confession of Faith of Those Churches which are commonly (though falsely) called Anabaptist." This document is Calvinistic and affirms believer's baptism by immersion. Estep comments, "For the first time Calvinism and Anabaptism merged to produce a new and different religious configuration in seventeenth-century England."[10] Thus these first-generation Particular Baptists embraced the three pillars of a developing new covenant theology: the Christ-centered biblical storyline, the believers-only church and the doctrines of grace. To further clarify this position, Benjamin Fox republished this confession in 1946 with an appendix at the end.

THE FIRST LONDON CONFESSION OF FAITH, 1646 EDITION, WITH AN APPENDIX BY BENJAMIN COX

Article X

JESUS Christ is made the mediator of the new and everlasting covenant of grace between God and Man, ever to be perfectly

---

8   Erroll Hulse, *An Introduction to the Baptists*, 2nd ed. (Haywards Heath, England: Carey, 1976), 25.

9   William R. Estep, *The Anabaptist Story*, rev. ed. 1975, 229.

10 Ibid., 229.

and fully the prophet, priest, and king of the Church of God for evermore (emphasis Long's).[11]

The new covenant is the everlasting covenant promised in Scripture. When Jesus came as the mediator of that covenant, he fulfilled perfectly and fully the offices of Prophet, Priest and King. This is not the covenant of grace as taught by covenant theologians. Maxcey writes:

> Like the Westminster Divines, first-generation seventeenth-century English Particular Baptists believed that the Scriptures set forth two covenants: a "covenant of works" and a "covenant of grace." However, they understood the "covenant of grace" to be the New Covenant, an absolute covenant, and the "covenant of works" to be the Old Covenant, a conditional covenant. As Patient wrote: "Now if any please but to search these Scriptures [Heb. 8:6–7] *it will appear that there [are] two real distinct Covenants or Testaments, the one of Grace, and the other of works, the one conditional, the other absolute*" (emphasis Maxcey's).[12]

Article XIII declares that no one else is qualified to be our Prophet, Priest and King, including Moses:

Article XIII

THIS office to be mediator, that is, to be prophet, priest, and king of the Church of God, is so proper to Christ, that neither in whole, or any part thereof, it cannot be transferred from Him to any other (emphasis Long's).[13]

---

11 *The First London Confession of Faith, 1646 Edition* (Belton, TX: Sovereign Grace Ministries, 2004), 5.

12 Patient, *The Doctrine of Baptism, and the Distinction of the Covenants or a Plain Treatise, Wherein the Four Essentials of Baptism Are Diligently Handled* (London: 1654), 30; cited by Zachary Maxcey, "Historical Forerunners of New Covenant Theology," Part 2 of 3, *Providence Theological Seminary Journal*, no. 2 (February 2014): 14, 15. Patient is one of the pastors who signed the First London Confession of Faith.

13 *The First London Confession of Faith, 1646 Edition*, 5, 6.

Article XXV declares that Christ saves sinners directly. Conversion does not first require a ministry of Moses' Law:

Article XXV

THE preaching of the gospel to the conversion of sinners, is absolutely free, no way requiring as absolutely necessary, any qualifications, preparations, or terrors of the law, or preceding ministry of the law, but only and alone the naked soul, a sinner and ungodly, to receive Christ crucified, dead and buried, and risen again; who is made a prince and a Savior for such sinners as through the gospel shall be brought to believe on Him (emphasis Long's).[14]

Article XXIX declares that, as King, Christ is the lawgiver of the church. Sanctification is a spiritual grace through which believers gradually obey more fully Christ's commands:

Article XXIX

ALL believers are a holy and sanctified people, and that sanctification is a spiritual grace of the new covenant, and an effect of the love of God manifested in the soul, whereby the believer presseth after a heavenly and evangelical obedience to all the commands, which Christ as head and king in His new covenant has prescribed to them (emphasis Long's).[15]

Article XXXIII declares that the church consists only of regenerated believers—not a mixture of believers and non-believers:

Article XXXIII

JESUS Christ hath here on earth a [manifestation of His] spiritual kingdom, which is His Church, whom He hath purchased and redeemed to Himself, as a peculiar inheritance; which Church is a company of visible saints, called and separated from the world by the word and Spirit of God, to the visible

---

14 Ibid., 10.
15 Ibid., 11.

profession of faith of the gospel, being baptized into that faith, and joined to the Lord, and each other, by mutual agreement in the practical enjoyment of the ordinances commanded by Christ their head and king (emphasis Long's).[16]

Article XXXIX declares the correct order of events: faith in Christ for salvation, followed by believer's baptism, then the Lord's Supper:

Article XXXIX

BAPTISM is an ordinance of the New Testament, given by Christ, to be dispensed upon persons professing faith, or that are made disciples; who upon profession of faith, ought to be baptized, and after to partake of the Lord's Supper (emphasis Long's).[17]

Article XL declares that the body of the person being baptized must be immersed under water:

Article XL

THAT the way and manner of the dispensing this ordinance, is dipping or plunging the body under water; it being a sign, must answer the things signified, which is, that interest the saints have in the death, burial, and resurrection of Christ… (emphasis Long's).[18]

Benjamin Cox wrote an Appendix to this 1646 Baptist Confession of Faith: "Published for the further clearing of Truth, and discovery of their mistake who have imagined a dissent in fundamentals when there is none."[19] In Article IX, Cox declares that believers are free from Moses' Law. Nevertheless we are under the law of Christ:

---

16 Ibid., 12, 13.

17 Ibid., 14.

18 Ibid., 15.

19 Ibid., 23.

Appendix: Article IX

Though we that believe in Christ be not under the law, but under grace, Rom. 6:14; yet we know that we are not lawless, or left to live without a rule; "not without law to God, but under law to Christ," I Cor. 9:21. The Gospel of Jesus Christ is a law, or commanding rule unto us; whereby, and in obedience whereunto, we are taught to live soberly, righteously, and godly in this present world, Titus 2: 11, 12; the directions of Christ in His evangelical word guiding us unto, and in this sober, righteous, and godly walking, I Tim. 1:10, 11.[20]

In Article X, Cox explains that believers interpret Moses' Law through the eyes of Christ. Because God never changes, we may glean principles for living from a new covenant perspective in the Law of Moses.

Appendix: Article X

Though we be not now sent to the law as it was in the hand of Moses, to be commanded thereby, yet Christ in His Gospel teacheth and commandeth us to walk in the same way of righteousness and holiness that God by Moses did command the Israelites to walk in, all the commandments of the Second Table being still delivered unto us by Christ, and all the commandments of the First Table also (as touching the life and spirit of them) in this epitome or brief sum, "Thou shalt love the Lord thy God with all thine heart, etc. "[21]

In 1662, Charles II granted royal assent to an Act of Uniformity. Clergymen had to plead allegiance to the revised Prayer Book of the Church of England or face penalties. By 1664, dissenters suffered much persecution. As Calvinists, the Particular Baptists felt closer to the Presbyterians and Congregationalists than to the General Baptists who taught free will in salvation. In 1677, they drafted The Second London Confession, a revision of the

---

20 Ibid., 27.

21 Ibid., 27, 28.

Presbyterians' Westminster Confession, and signed it in 1689. The Baptists copied the language of the covenant theologians almost word for word, but corrected differences on believer's baptism, church government, the role of civil magistrates, and the biblical storyline.

The Baptists retained the teaching of the Westminster Confession with regard to three covenants: those of redemption, works, and grace. Yet there was one important distinction. Covenant theology teaches that the covenant of grace forms an arch over all the biblical covenants. In so doing, they flat line Scripture so that the new covenant is not really new but renewed.[22] The old covenant and the new covenant become two administrations or applications of the covenant of grace. In contrast, the Baptists deleted the two sections, which explained how God worked in two different administrations, effectively denying the storyline of covenant theologians. Instead they viewed redemptive history as gradually progressing to Christ. They wrote, "This covenant is revealed through the Gospel; first of all to Adam in the promise of salvation by the seed of the woman, and afterwards by further steps until the full revelation of it became complete in the New Testament."[23] Thus the words "covenant theology" and "covenant of grace" meant one thing to Particular Baptists but something different to Presbyterians.[24]

Regarding the nature of God's law, these second-generation Particular Baptists aligned themselves with the Presbyterians and agreed to the tripartite division of the Law given to

---

22 A. Blake White, *The Newness of the New Covenant*, 5.

23 "God's Covenant," in *The Baptist Confession of Faith (1689)*, 12, article 7 no. 3, revised by C. H. Spurgeon, last modified (date), accessed February 23, 2008, http://www.spurgeon.org//~phil/creeds/bcof.htm.

24 Heather A. Kendall, "The Bible's Storyline: How It Affects the Doctrine of Salvation," 64.

Moses into moral, ceremonial and civil commands. The Ten Commandments became the unchanging moral law of God. Thus the Law of Moses had more authority than the law of Christ for the believer. Jesus is the lawgiver of the new covenant in the First London Confession of Faith.[25] However, the Second London Confession of 1689 copies the Westminster Confession.

According to the Westminster Confession, Christ does not have any authority to change the moral law of God as given to Moses. New covenant theologians view Jesus as our King with authority over the whole of creation, and especially over the church (Matthew 28: 18–20). To allow Moses authority over Christ downgrades the supremacy of Christ. As we shall see later in this history, this view became the central issue between Reformed Baptists and Sovereign Grace Baptists—those believers who objected to the covenant of grace as taught by the Presbyterians. Article 19, of the Second London Confession of 1689, illustrates how a covenant theology storyline of Scripture elevates Moses' authority over Christ:

THE SECOND BAPTIST LONDON CONFESSION OF 1689

19. The Law of God

1. God gave to Adam a law of universal obedience which was written in his heart...

2. The same Law that was first written in the heart of man, continued to be a perfect rule of righteousness after the Fall, and was delivered by God upon Mount Sinai in the ten commandments and written in two Tables...

---

25 See Article XXV and XXIX in the 1646 Baptist Confession—also, Appendix: Article IX and Appendix: X in Benjamin Cox's Appendix to the Confession.

7. Besides this law commonly called moral law, God was pleased to give the people of Israel ceremonial laws containing several typical ordinances.

9. The moral Law ever binds to obedience everyone, justified people as well as others, and not only in regard of the matter contained in it, but also out of respect for the authority of God the Creator, Who gave the law. Nor does Christ in the Gospel dissolve this law in any way, but He considerably strengthens our obligation to obey it.[26]

ENGLISH PREACHERS DISPLAYING GLIMPSES OF A DEVELOPING NEW COVENANT THEOLOGY

The following preachers suffered persecution because they exalted Christ over Moses. As a result others accused them of being Antinomian.[27]

TOBIAS CRISP, 1600–1643

Some clergymen accused Crisp, a Church of England clergyman, of being Antinomian because he exalted Christ in his preaching. Note that he preached before the Particular Baptists broke away from the congregational churches. To defend false accusations that free grace encourages licentiousness, he preached the following sermon:

> But some will say, By this it seems we take away all endeavors and employment from believers, the free-men of Christ. Doth

---

26 "The Law of God," in *The Baptist Confession of Faith (1689)*, 24, 25.

27 The New Lexicon Webster's Encylopedic Dictionary defines antinomian: 1. *adj.* denying that one is bound to obey the moral law 2. *n.* someone who adhered to the view, esp. put forward during the Reformation, that Christians are justified by faith alone and that salvation does not depend upon obedience to the moral law. (fr. Gk *anti-*, against + *nomos*, law). *The New Lexicon Webster's Dictionary of the English Language*, Canadian Edition (New York, NY: Lexicon, 1988), 40.

Christ do everything for them? Do they stand righteous before God, in respect of what he hath done for them? Then they may sit still: they may do what they list.

I answer, Will you deny this, that we are righteous with and that we are righteous with God by the righteousness of Christ? Or is it by our own righteousness? Then mark what the apostle saith, "They (saith he, speaking of the Jews), going about to establish their own righteousness, have not submitted themselves to the righteousness of God, for Christ is the end of the law for righteousness, to every one that believeth," (Rom. 10:3, 4). Either you must disclaim Christ's righteousness, [or] you must disclaim your own; for, if the gift of God "be of grace, then it is not of works, else work is no more work; and, if it be of works, it is no more of grace, otherwise grace is no more grace," (Rom. 11:6).

But you will say further to me (for, except a man be a mere Papist, I am sure he cannot deny but that the righteousness by which I stand righteous before God, is the righteousness Christ doth for me, and not that I do for myself), you will ask me, I say, Doth not this take off all manner of obedience and all manner of holiness?

…We have justification, our peace, our salvation, only by the righteousness Christ hath done for us: but this doth not take away our obedience, nor our services, in respect of those ends for which such are now required of believers. We have yet several ends for duties and obedience, namely, That they may glorify God, and evidence our thankfulness, that they may be profitable to men that they may be ordinances wherein to meet with God, to make good what he hath promised….and, in regard of such ends, there is a gracious freedom that the free-men of Christ have by him; that is, so far forth as services and obediences are expected at the free-man's hand, for the ends that I have named, there is Christ, by his Spirit, present with those that are free-men, to help them in all such kind of services, so that "they become strong in the Lord, and in the power of his might," to do the will of God. Mark what the apostle speaks: "I am able to do all things through Christ that strengthens me. Of

myself (saith he) I am able to do nothing; but with Christ, and
through him that strengthens me, I am able to do all things."
He that is Christ's free-man hath always the strength of Christ
present, answerable to that weight and burden of employment
God calls him forth unto.[28]

JOHN OWEN, 1616–1683

Owen was a Congregationalist preacher and theologian who lived
during the English civil war (1642—1649). For a short time he
became a member of Cromwell's parliament. Congregationalists
were Puritans who wanted to reform the Church of England.
Although a covenant theologian, Owen expressed some ideas
similar to NCT. The following quotes mean that the old covenant is not another administration of the over-arching "covenant of grace." Owen recognized that the old covenant required
perfect obedience and connected it to the covenant of works
with Adam—unlike most covenant theologians. Therefore the
old covenant was not based on grace and was only a temporary
picture or type of the permanent new covenant.

> God had before given the covenant of works, or perfect obedi-
> ence, to all mankind, in the law of creation. But this covenant
> at Sinai did not abrogate or disannul that covenant, nor in any
> way fulfill it. And the reason is, because it was never intended
> to come in the place or room of it, as a covenant, containing an
> entire rule of all the faith and obedience of the whole church.
> God did not intend in it to abrogate the covenant of works,
> and to substitute this in the place of it; yea in various things it
> reinforced, established, and confirmed that covenant.[29]

---

28 Tobias Crisp, "Christian Liberty No Licentious Doctrine," last modified
    (date), accessed March 30, 2015, http://www.pbministries.org/Theology/
    Crisp,Tobias/sermon8.htm.

29 John Owen, "An exposition of Hebrews 8:6-13: Wherein, The Nature
    and Differences between the Old and New Covenants is discovered,"
    cited in *Covenant Theology: From Adam to Christ*, ed. Ronald D. Millar,

Owen also wrote, "They differ in their substance and end. The old covenant was typical, shadowy, and removable, Heb. 10:1. The new covenant is substantial and permanent, as containing the body, which is Christ. Now, consider the old covenant comparatively with the new, and this part of its nature, that is typical and shadowy, is a great debasement of it."[30]

JOHN BUNYAN, 1628–1688

John Bunyan was a non-conformist Baptist preacher who spent twelve years in jail after the restoration of the English monarchy in 1660. Concerning the relationship of Moses' Law to the Christian, he wrote:

> 4. From all which I gather, that, though as to the matter of the law, both as to its being given the first time and the second, it binds the unbeliever under the pains of eternal damnation (if he close not with Christ by faith); yet as to the manner of its giving at these two times, I think the first doth more principally intend its force as a covenant of works, not at all respecting the Lord Jesus; but this second time not (at least in the manner of its being given) respecting such a covenant, but rather as a rule or directory to those who already are found in the clift of the rock Christ; for the saint himself, though he be without law to God, as it is considered the first or old covenant, yet even he is not without law to him as considered under grace; not without law to God, but under the law to Christ.
>
> 5. Though, therefore, it be sad with the unbeliever, because he only and wholly standeth under the law as it is given in fire, in smoke, in blackness, and darkness, and thunder; all which threaten him with eternal ruin if he fulfil not the utmost tittle

James M. Renihan, and Francisco Orozco (Palmdale, CA: Reformed Baptist Academic Press, 2005), 188; cited by Zachary Maxcey, "Historical Forerunners of New Covenant Theology," Part 3 of 3, *Providence Theological Seminary Journal*, no. 3 (May 2015): 8.

30 Ibid., 8.

thereof; yet the believer stands to the law under no such consideration, neither is he so at all to hear or regard it, for he is now removed from thence to the blessed mountain of Zion—to grace and forgiveness of sins; he is now, I say, by faith in the Lord Jesus, shrouded under so perfect and blessed a righteousness, that this thundering law of Mount Sinai cannot find the least fault or diminution therein, but rather approveth and alloweth thereof, either when or wherever it find it. This is called the righteousness of God without the law, and also said to be witnessed by both the law and the prophets; even the righteousness of God, which is by faith in Jesus Christ unto all and upon all them that believe; for there is no difference.

6. Wherefore, whenever thou who believest in Jesus, dost hear the law in its thundering and lightning fits, as if it would burn up heaven and earth, then say thou, I am freed from this law, these thunderings have nothing to do with my soul; nay, even this law, while it thus thunders and roars, it doth both allow and approve of my righteousness. I know that Hagar would sometimes be domineering and high, even in Sarah's house, and against her; but this she is not to be suffered to do, nay, though Sarah herself be barren; wherefore, serve it also as Sarah served her, and expel her out from thy house. My meaning is, when this law with its thundering threatenings doth attempt to lay hold on thy conscience, shut it out with a promise of grace; cry, The inn is taken up already; the Lord Jesus is here entertained, and here is no room for the law. Indeed, if it will be content with being my informer, and so lovingly leave off to judge me, I will be content, it shall be in my sight, I will also delight therein; but otherwise, I being now made upright without it, and that too with that righteousness which this law speaks well of and approveth, I may not, will not, cannot dare not make it my Saviour and judge, nor suffer it to set up its government in my conscience; for by so doing, I fall from grace, and Christ Jesus doth profit me nothing. [31]

---

31 John Bunyan, *Of the Law and the Christian*, last modified (date), accessed January 7, 2015, http://solochristo.com/theology/nct/ JohnBunyan_LawandtheChristian.html.

JOHN GILL, 1697–1771

John Gill was a Strict Baptist[32] who taught, "The Son of God…is King of saints, and Lawgiver in his house, and has given out commandments to be observed, and laws of discipline for the right ordering of his house…and particularly the new commandment of love, which is eminently called the law of Christ."[33]

WILLIAM HUNTINGTON, 1745–1813

A Baptist and an independent preacher, Huntington was falsely accused of being Antinomian because he taught that believers are under the law of Christ.

"Now therefore why tempt ye God, to put a yoke upon the neck of the disciples, which neither our fathers nor we were able to bear?" The liberty which Peter here alludes to is the liberty of the Holy Spirit, which God had given them, which Paul calls the law of the Spirit of life, which made him free from the law of sin and death; and "where the Spirit of the Lord is there is liberty," (2 Cor.3:17) for, as David says, the Spirit of God is a free Spirit. (Psa. 2:12) The rule that Peter gives them is faith, which purifies the heart. The unbearable yoke that they were going to tempt God with, by galling the neck of the disciples, was first, the needfulness of circumcision; Secondly, a command to keep the law of Moses; and it is called tempting God, because it was a reflection cast upon His work who had purified their hearts by

---

32 During the first half of the 18th century, some Particular Baptists became hyper-Calvinists and separated to form the Strict Baptists. They denied that saving faith was the duty of unbelievers; communion should be restricted to those believers of the same faith and order; the Gospel, not the moral law, is the rule of life for the believer. Errol Hulse lists those three tenets of the Strict Baptists on the front cover of his book, *An Introduction to the Baptists.*

33 John Gill, *Body of Divinity*, Vol. 2, 798; cited by Jon Zens, "'This is My Beloved Son…Hear Him': A Study of the Development of Law in the History of Redemption," *Baptist Reformation Review*, 7, no. 4 (Winter 1978): 26.

faith, and sent His Spirit to govern and lead them into all truth; as if the Holy Spirit was not sufficient to make them obedient, nor God's purifying their hearts a sufficient purification, nor faith a sufficient rule, without yoking them with the killing letter as the only rule of life.

The law obeyed, and disarmed of its curse, is in the heart of the Mediator, who is Judge of quick and dead, and therefore keeps the keys of hell and of death. The believer is under the law of faith to Christ; and they that are His have crucified the flesh with the affections and lusts; such are delivered from the law; and against such there is no law; and sin is not imputed where there is no law. I do insist upon it that, if a believer be brought to the law of Moses, to be under it in any other sense, sin stares him in the face, wrath works in his heart, his enmity is stirred up, bondage seizes him, and despondency or despair will sink him, unless the law of the Spirit of life makes him free from the law of sin and death.[34]

WILLIAM MASON, 1773

Many condemned William Mason, a theologian and writer in the Church of England, for being an Antinomian because he focused solely on Christ for his justification and sanctification. He responded:

Me thinks I find myself such an infinite debtor to my Lord, for his matchless love, rich grace, and glorious salvation, that I never would have done testifying of him to my fellow sinners, while my heart can beat, my tongue can speak, or my hand can write....

However, I think it behoves me to embrace this opportunity, to testify, that if for declaring that the justification of sinners, from first to last, is by the free grace of God, through the life and death, the one atonement, and the one righteousness of the Son of God, without any of our works and deservings—...If we do not hate sin, which

---

34 William Huntington, last modified (date), accessed March 26, 2015, http://users.rcn.com/delong/williamh.html.

once we loved, and love holiness which once we hated, we have no evidence that we possess the faith of God's elect. That faith by which salvation is now enjoyed, and to which eternal life is forever secured in Christ Jesus —for Christ is to all who believe, as precious as a Saviour from the power of sin, as he is a Justifier from the condemnation for sin. Now, I say, if for believing and contending for these scriptural truths, I am deemed an Antinomian, I pray God I may increase and abound herein more and more, and live and die in such blessed antinomianism (italics Mason's).[35]

---

35 William Mason, *The Believer's Pocket Companion: The One Thing needful To Make Poor Sinners Rich & Miserable Sinners Happy*, first pub. 1773 (Willow Street, PA: Old Paths Publications, 2000), ii–v.

CHAPTER 4

LAYING THE GROUNDWORK: THE DOCTRINES OF GRACE (FROM THE LATE 1940s)

I have spent a lot of time so far describing the problem with the storyline of covenant theology. In flat lining Scripture, covenant theologians downgraded the supremacy of Christ over Moses. They also allowed a mixed multitude of believers and non-believers in the church. In contrast, we saw some theologians who preferred to view the redemptive storyline of Scripture as progressive-historical, culminating in Christ. Other theologians also believed in a believers-only church. Those beliefs are two of the pillars of NCT.

The third pillar of NCT is a belief in the doctrines of grace. Throughout this book I have been stating that covenant theology and dispensationalism misrepresent the relationship between the Testaments. Correctly putting the Testaments together is the main concern of NCT. A belief in the doctrines of grace does not affect this storyline. Nevertheless this chapter will explain how a belief in the doctrines of grace laid the groundwork for this modern movement. The NCT movement began like a tiny mustard seed that is continuing to grow into a large tree founded on the doctrines of grace.

John Calvin first published the *Institutes of the Christian Religion* in 1536 and the final edition in 1559. This book defines the most thorough and popular presentation of Protestant doctrine produced by anyone in the Reformation. In considering predestination, Calvin writes:

> Now, if we are not really ashamed of the Gospel, we must of necessity acknowledge what is therein openly declared: that God by His eternal goodwill (for which there was no other cause than His own purpose), appointed those whom He pleased unto salvation, rejecting all the rest; and that those whom He blessed with this free adoption to be His sons He illumines by His Holy Spirit, that they may receive the life which is offered to them in Christ; while others, continuing of their own will in unbelief, are left destitute of the light of faith, in total darkness.[1]

The Puritans and independent preachers in England, even those who opposed covenant theology's storyline, all believed in Calvin's views on predestination. Thus the roots of NCT include a belief in God's sovereignty in salvation. The phrase, doctrines of grace, became a modern way of defining Calvin's beliefs. In the late 1940s and 1950s, God raised up preachers in the United States who began embracing God's sovereignty in salvation— men like Rolfe Barnard, S. Lewis Johnson, Ernie Reisinger, and John G. Reisinger. In 1963, Southern Baptist preachers, David N. Steele and Curtis C. Thomas, co-authored a book which popularized the acronym TULIP: total depravity, unconditional election, limited atonement, irresistible grace, and perseverance of the saints. The doctrines of grace are at the root of the

---

1   John Calvin, *A Treatise on the Eternal Predestination of God*, translated by Henry Cole, in *Calvin's Calvinism* (Grand Rapids, MI: Eerdmans, 1950), 31; cited by R. C. Sproul, *What is Reformed Theology?: Understanding the Basics* (Grand Rapids, MI: Baker Books, 1997), 158, 159.

sovereign grace movement. Years later, Sovereign Grace Baptist churches would become the vehicle in which NCT would flourish. John Reisinger, a Baptist pastor from Pennsylvania, would become a driving force in promoting NCT.

ROLFE BARNARD, 1904–1969

When eleven, Barnard appeared to accept Christ at a missionary meeting in a Southern Baptist church. Inwardly, however, he remained a rebellious sinner. Strangely, although he was not saved, Barnard still sensed God wanted him to become a preacher. Nevertheless he resisted God so that during university in Texas he became president of an atheist's club. His mother, however, continued to believe God would call her son to be a preacher.

After graduation, he became a school teacher in Texas. At that time teachers there had to be church members. Since Barnard had enough Bible knowledge to teach a men's class, the church leadership allowed him to do this. Unbeknownst to him, they knew he was not saved. His mother had written a letter to the church with a prayer request: "My boy's coming to your town to teach school. He's called to be a preacher. He's not even saved. He's in an awful mess. If you could find it in your heart, build a fire under him. Don't let him have a moment's peace."[2] Eventually, God answered his mother's prayer. As soon as Barnard surrendered to the Lord, he did begin preaching.

In 1928, Barnard became a student at Southwestern Baptist Seminary in Fort Worth, Texas. One of his professors was Dr. W. T. Conner, a Calvinist. Yet, after graduation, he routinely gave

---

2   Roger Fay, "Rolfe Barnard (1904–1969)," 1, last modified (date), accessed January 8, 2015, http://www.reformation-today.org/articles/Rolfe_Barnard_(1904–1969).pdf.

altar calls during those early years as an itinerant evangelist. In 1946, he began teaching at Piedmont College in North Carolina where he met Dr. John R. Rice. Then, in the late 1940s, he "happened" to purchase a second-hand book of sermons by B. H. Carroll. One sentence from a sermon on John 5:25 "ruined" his ministry. Roger Fay, a Reformed Baptist author, explains:

> He [Barnard] restudied Conner, the Puritans and Reformers and came to the settled conviction that sovereign grace was the message of the Bible. He began to preach his new discoveries. The defining moment then came at the Fundamentalist "Sword of the Lord" Conference at Tocoa Falls, Georgia, in 1949. The conference was dedicated to soul-winning techniques. The speakers were Dr. John Rice, Lee Robertson, Bill Rice, E. J. Daniels and Rolfe Barnard.
>
> Barnard was to be first. When he began preaching he asked all the young preachers to open their Bibles to Romans 9 and all the old preachers to keep theirs shut, since they would not believe anything he was going to say! Everyone opened their Bibles! He preached for an hour on sovereign grace and it is reported that by the next morning the conference was in turmoil. By the middle of the week Dr. Rice had asked Barnard to leave.[3]

Evidently Rice was not expecting Barnard to preach a fiery evangelistic sermon on sovereign grace, based on Romans 9. According to Reformed Baptist pastors, Thomas Chantry and David Dykstra:

> Barnard was branded among southern fundamentalists as a dangerous man, and fewer opportunities would come his way....
>
> The following year, however, he was invited to preach at a "revival" in Ashland, Kentucky. There he met Henry Mahan, a newly called assistant pastor. Barnard preached again on the sovereignty of God, this time from Romans 8:28. His preaching had a great effect on Mahan, who, as pastor of the Thirteenth

---

3   Ibid., 2.

Street Baptist Church in Ashland, would become the sponsor of the Sovereign Grace Bible Conference beginning in 1954. Through the ministry of Barnard and Mahan at the Ashland conference a group of Calvinistic Baptists began to grow—first in Ohio and Kentucky and later beyond.[4]

While a Baptist seminary student, Mark McCulley writes about Barnard's preaching:

> Though Barnard was a well-educated man, he had a simple message which he shouted at the top of his voice: *Christ is Lord, not just Savior*; Christ does not owe anybody anything; and revival comes by the Holy Spirit, not by man's manipulations and programs. Or, as he would say about Rom. 8:28—"God does things on purpose!" Though his methods were radical, Rolfe Barnard saw many converts come to Christ....
>
> It would be wrong, however, to imply that Rolfe Barnard's main concern was to make Calvinists out of Arminians. He was not interested in scholastic quibbling. Shockingly honest about the absence of revival in his life and in the places where he preached, Barnard longed for the presence and power of Christ in local churches....
>
> Rolfe's methods were unusual *because* he mistrusted the programmed professionalism which had lost the sense of expectancy and dependency on the Holy Spirit to work. With great sorrow, Barnard would exclaim: "I'm sorry, but it's true. The men *we* get saved don't *stay* saved. Only the *Lord* can change men's hearts" (italics McCulley's).[5]

Fay also comments on Barnard's preaching:

> Barnard once preached on "Six stubborn statements". His hearers had to face these facts—God is absolutely sovereign in all

---

4   Thomas Chantry and David Dykstra, *Holding Communion Together, The Reformed Baptists: The First Fifty Years, Divided & United* (Birmingham, AL: Solid Ground Christian Books, 2014), 69.

5   Mark McCulley, *Studies in History and Ethics* (Malin, OR: BREM, 1982), 23.

things or he is not, he can't be both. Man is totally dead as a result of the fall or he is not, he can't merely be wounded. Almighty God predestined to save a people or he didn't; Jesus Christ effectually redeemed all his people on the cross; salvation is by divine revelation (Matt 16); all God's people are going to persevere to the end. This was typical of his preaching. Not that Rolfe ignored the freeness of God's grace. He was emphatic that all his hearers' duty was to respond to his message; he would sometimes literally beg them to turn to Christ.[6]

Years later, Norbert Ward, who founded the *Baptist Reformation Review* in 1972, worked as a sound engineer at CBS Records in Nashville, Tennessee. In 1976, he compiled many of Rolfe Barnard's sermons and created several LP albums so that more people could hear them.

S. LEWIS JOHNSON

Lewis Johnson was working in the insurance business when God saved him in Birmingham, Alabama. In 1943, he enrolled in Dallas Theological Seminary and graduated in 1949 with a Th.D. He became a professor of New Testament and later a professor of systematic theology at Dallas Seminary after he had graduated. He was the pastor for many years at Believers Chapel in Dallas, Texas. Although he passed away in 2004, his influence still lives on, thanks to the generosity of the Believers Chapel; for they still make available almost 1500 of his sermons downloadable for free on their website. Phil Johnson, a church historian, writes:

> My first exposure to Johnson's preaching was about two decades ago—maybe more. Someone gave me his tapes on the doctrines of grace. The clarity with which he dealt with the extent-of-the-atonement issue settled some questions I had been grappling

---

6   Roger Fay, "Rolfe Barnard (1904–1969)," 5.

with for a long time. What I appreciated most was Johnson's *biblical* approach. Those tapes changed my whole perspective on the relationship between systematic doctrine and biblical exposition. They also marked a major turning point in my thinking about Calvinism, Arminianism, and biblical soteriology.

Dr. Johnson did not publish a large body of written material, but his sermons have been disseminated freely for years by the tape ministry of Believers Chapel (Dallas)....Those sermons may be a more valuable legacy than a shelf full of popular-level books would have been. For someone like me, who never went to seminary, it's great to have so much solid teaching from a premier seminary professor (italics Johnson's).[7]

Lewis Johnson, along with Ferrell Griswold,[8] was one of only a few preachers in the southern United States who taught the doctrines of grace and remained isolated from mainstream Baptists in the 1950s and 1960s.

REFORMED BAPTISTS AND SOVEREIGN GRACE BAPTISTS

Many Baptists who believed in God's sovereignty in salvation began to read literature from the Puritans. When they discovered how their Baptist forefathers had embraced the London Confession of 1689, some of them decided to form churches around that confession. They called themselves, Reformed Baptists. Others, who preferred the London Confession of 1644 or 1646, called themselves Sovereign Grace Baptists.

---

7   Phil Johnson, "Here's a real gold mine," 1, 2, last modified (date), accessed January 22, 2015, http://teampyro.blogspot.ca/2006/03/heres-real-gold-mine.html.

8   Ferrell Griswold (1928–1982) earned his Master's degree at Grace Seminary in Albany, Georgia, and his Doctor's degree at the University of Chicago. Although a pastor in Birmingham, Alabama, he lectured and preached in many places around the world on the doctrines of grace. One may still hear his audio sermons on the Internet.

The Reformed Baptist, Steve Martin, describes his Baptist heritage:

> By the 1950s, some Baptists, disillusioned with Dispensational theology and fundamentalism's "easy believism," refusing to believe that Barthian theology was an improvement over liberalism, began to see in Scripture and history the old wells of theology from which their ancestors had drunk deeply and which changed their lives and their nations. They wanted both the doctrines of grace of the Protestant Reformation, but also the evangelical and Baptistic doctrines of their Puritan Baptist forefathers.
>
> In the 1960s, Baptists began to adopt the 2nd London Confession of 1689 as their understanding of the Bible and its theology. Baptist churches in the Mid-Atlantic States of Pennsylvania, New Jersey and New York began to form around the 1689 Confession, holding family conferences, pastors' conferences and publishing materials consistent with their theology. The Banner of Truth placed its North American headquarters in Carlisle, Pennsylvania, largely through the impetus of Reformed Baptist Ernie Reisinger and Grace Baptist Church of Carlisle.[9]

The Banner of Truth is a United Kingdom organization governed by the Westminster Confession of Faith. In 1978, when Ernest Reisinger became a trustee of that organization, he became the official host for the US Banner of Truth Conferences at his church in Carlisle, Pennsylvania. For many years the Sovereign Grace Baptists and the Reformed Baptists enjoyed each other's fellowship. "When the Banner of Truth began sponsoring Ministers Conferences in the US in 1978, Calvinistic Baptists of various stripes enjoyed fellowship there."[10]

---

9   Steve Martin, "A Brief History of Reformed Baptists," 2, last modified (date), accessed March 16, 2014, http://www.reformedbaptist.org/who-we-are/a-brief-history-of-reformed-baptists.

10 Thomas Chantry and David Dykstra, *Holding Communion Together*, 70.

DAVID N. STEELE AND CURTIS C. THOMAS

God also used David N. Steele and Curtis C. Thomas as seeds of the NCT movement. Steele has passed away, but I talked to Curtis Thomas. He was seventeen years old and unsaved when a gentleman asked his brother if he could study the Scriptures with him. His brother refused, but Thomas accepted the invitation. About six or eight people met to study Romans. Although Thomas had no prior Bible knowledge, God used Romans 1:17 to save him: "The just shall live by faith." Immediately he saw election in the Scriptures.

In 1963, Steele and Thomas were co-pastors of a Southern Baptist church in Little Rock, Arkansas. That same year the Presbyterian and Reformed Publishing Company published their two books, *Romans: An Interpretive Outline* and *The Five Points of Calvinism*. Kenneth J. Stewart, professor of theological studies, comments:

> Many can remember initially encountering the points of Calvinism through the large booklet of the writers, Steele and Thomas. When in 1963, David N. Steele and Curtis C. Thomas released their *The Five Points of Calvinism Defined, Defended, Documented* and in the process helped to popularize the TULIP acronym, a reader might easily have supposed that they were relaying a formula of considerable vintage. Steele and Thomas apparently believed so, and it appears that they were in good company. The renowned Reformation historian, the late Lewis W. Spitz of Stanford University (and formerly of Concordia Seminary, St. Louis) though he disapproved of the acronym, spoke of it in 1971 as by then a "familiar caricature of Calvin's theology."…
>
> But to return to Steele and Thomas, the intriguing thing one finds on reading their booklet closely is that of the older works on Calvinist history and theology which they relied upon in their preparation to write on this subject, only *one* utilized the

TULIP acronym....The one clear source drawn on by Steele and Thomas which *did* employ the TULIP acronym was Loraine Boettner's *The Reformed Doctrine of Predestination* (1932). Evidently then, Steele and Thomas were not the originators of TULIP but only among its most successful popularizers; the acronym has a shadowy history extending back to Boettner's utilization of it, and perhaps beyond (italics Stewart's).[11]

The popularity of Steele and Thomas' book is significant for two reasons pertinent to this history. First, they were pastors in the Southern Baptist Convention. Tom Nettles, a professor and historian, writes, "The story of the commitment of early Baptists to the doctrines of grace is a picture of unity and fortitude. The earliest Baptist in America, Roger Williams, was a decided Calvinist and built his theory of religious liberty on his commitment to total depravity, unconditional election, effectual calling, perseverance of the saints, and definite atonement."[12]

Moreover Nettles writes, "No one of trend-setting influence seriously challenged the Calvinistic hegemony before the arrival of E. Y. Mullins as president of the Southern Baptist Theological Seminary in 1899...The clear and precise commitment of Southern Baptists to Calvinism diminished rapidly after the time of Mullins. Preachers and teachers began to dismiss even the remnants of Calvinism remaining in Mullins."[13]

Steele and Thomas' books stood in sharp contrast to the man-centered free will theology of the Southern Baptists; for

---

11 Kenneth J. Stewart, "The Points of Calvinism: Retrospect and Prospect," 189, 190, last modified (date), accessed March 13, 2014, http://responsivereiding.files.wordpress.com/2009/03/points-of-calvinism-retrospect-and-prospect1.pdf.

12 Tom Nettles, "The Rise & Demise of Calvinism Among Southern Baptists," *Founders Journal*, 2, last modified (date), accessed January 25, 2014, http://www.founders.org/journal/fj19/article1.html.

13 Ibid., 10, 12.

no one else in the Southern Baptist Convention believed in the doctrines of grace at that time. While Reformed Baptists appreciated their work, Southern Baptists opposed it. Therefore Thomas left the Southern Baptist Convention and became an Independent Reformed Baptist pastor until he joined the Bible Church in Little Rock, Arkansas.

Secondly, Steele and Thomas divorced the doctrines of grace from covenant theology's hermeneutics of flat lining Scripture and putting Moses, or the old covenant, equal to Christ, or the new covenant. What an important step when considering the development of NCT! A seminary student, Richard Lucas' comments are relevant although written years later:

> As I previously mentioned, in my limited experience the T.U.L.I.P. acronym has taken on a role of huge significance in identifying those who self-describe themselves as Reformed. While it is something of an historical novelty, these New Calvinists have in mind, not necessarily a confessional or ecclesiological definition of being Reformed, but merely a soteriological understanding. To them, being a Calvinist is to embrace the 5 points of Calvinism, which they readily know by the TULIP acronym.[14]

In 1973, George W. Dollar, a pastor and church historian, lamented a rising awareness of Calvinism within Fundamentalist churches. Indeed, in the 1970s, the Southern Baptist Convention ousted many pastors and churches that endorsed the doctrines of grace. This illustrates the influence of Steele and Thomas. Dollar writes:

> In the last ten years a new threat has emerged within Fundamentalism itself. This has been militant and rigid Calvinism, usually expressed in its Five Points (TULIP), total

---

14 Richard Lucas, "Are you Reformed? (Part 2)," 1, last modified (date), accessed March 13, 2014, http://www.credomag.com/2012/07/27/are-you-reformed-part-2/.

depravity, unconditional election, limited atonement, irresistible grace, and perseverance of the saints. This system has long been an integral part of such churches as the Presbyterian, the colonial Congregational, and the Reformed, as well as a few Baptist churches of the Spurgeon type....

One small Baptist paper, *The Baptist Examiner*, published by John R. Gilpin at Ashland, Kentucky, keeps up a steady attack on all who will not accept the Five Points, and publishes only articles by those who do. Many Independents without any solid affiliation with the national fellowships are promoters of hardline Calvinism. Most Fundamentalists, had they been polled throughout their history, would have accepted the tenets of total depravity and perseverance of the saints, but the majority would have rejected limited atonement and irresistible grace. On the point of unconditional election they would have given the largest possible place to the work of grace, but would have allowed a place for man's will in accepting that grace.[15]

JOHN G. REISINGER

Although John Reisinger's mother was not a Christian at the time, she forced him to go to Sunday school as a child. Sadly, he never heard the Gospel at that church. As soon as he was old enough, he quit. The first person to explain the way of salvation to him was his older brother Ernie. At first John refused to accept the message. He even moved away from his home in Pennsylvania to St. Louis so that he would not have to listen to him. By the time he eventually moved back home both of his brothers had trusted the Lord. One evening Donald and Ernie took John to a meeting in Lancaster, Pennsylvania, where a butcher was preaching. That night the Holy Spirit convicted John of his sin, and he trusted in Jesus to save him.

---

15 George W. Dollar, *A History of Fundamentalism in America* (Greenville, SC: Bob Jones University Press, 1973), 276.

After graduating from Lancaster Bible College, he became a pastor at the Reformed Baptist Church in Lewisburg, Pennsylvania, where he met I. C. Herendeen, who had sold Christian books through his Bible Truth Depot in Swengel, Pennsylvania. In 1918 Herendeen had published *The Sovereignty of God* by Arthur W. Pink. Herendeen and Pink had also worked together as associate editors of a periodical, *Studies in Scriptures* from 1922 to 1953.[16] Pink introduced Herendeen to the doctrines of grace, who in turn taught Reisinger many years later.

John Reisinger wanted to publish books and booklets from the day he was converted. He started by printing Spurgeon's sermons on a mimeograph machine. Then in 1966, he began publishing *The Sword and Trowel*, a monthly newspaper, which lasted for over twenty years. At first Ron McKinney was the assistant editor although he became the senior editor in 1976. The main purpose of the newspaper was to teach the doctrines of grace.

In the 200th issue of *Sound of Grace*, Reisinger explains:

From the beginning of our entrance into publishing we have had very narrow goals. First, we were interested in publishing material that glorified God by teaching his sovereign grace....

Second, we wanted to publish the doctrines of grace in a manner that the "man in the pew" could understand....We have aimed at making theology both understandable and enjoyable. One of the comments I often receive, and might add, greatly appreciate is, "Pastor John, I so much appreciate your ability to make me understand difficult truths." God said, "Feed my sheep," he did not say, "Feed my giraffes." We strive to put the cookies on the lower shelves.[17]

---

16 Joel Rishel, "The Impact of A. W. Pink," 2, 3, last modified (date), accessed March 26, 2014 http://www.biblebaptistelmont.org/BBC/library/pink. html.

17 John G. Reisinger, "John Reisinger on the 200th Issue of Sound of Grace," *Sound of Grace*, no. 200, (September 2013): 2.

Concerning *The Sword and Trowel*, Reisinger states:

> Our first struggle was with Arminianism. When we first started publishing material on the five points of Calvinism, we lost a lot of friends. At that point in history there was not a single publishing house that was Calvinistic and Baptistic. *Sword and Trowel* and *Sound of Grace* was one of the significant factors that helped to start and establish the Reformed Baptist movement. This latter split over the teaching of New Covenant Theology at a very early stage.[18]

Years later, at the first John Bunyan Conference in 1981, Reisinger commented:

> We used to laugh at Bob Jones for banning books from being read and expelling students for reading *The Sword and Trowel*. We said, "If Bob Jones is so sure that he has the Scripture on his side, why does he not set down with those confused students and say, Let me show you what these verses really mean. Let's examine every argument these books and writers use. Better yet, we will invite one of them to lecture and then we will ask him questions and show where he is wrong"! Of course, we know why none of those things were ever done. We know why they had to appeal to the "big stick" of personal authority. They could not exegete their basic presuppositions from the Word of God and so they simply refused to discuss it![19]

---

18 Ibid., 2.

19 John G. Reisinger, "When Should a Christian Leave a Church?", 11, last modified (date), accessed March 31, 2014, http://solochristo.com/theology/Church/reiwh.htm.

CHAPTER 5

THE BEGINNING OF NEW COVENANT THEOLOGY (FROM 1977 TO 1983)

Between 1977 and 1983 a war of words erupted between Reformed Baptists and Sovereign Grace Baptists. This controversy became particularly painful because the seven men involved were fellow believers and good friends. In fact Ernie and John Reisinger were brothers. As Reformed Baptists, Walter Chantry, Al Martin and Ernie Reisinger followed the 1689 London Baptist Confession of Faith. In contrast, Gary Long, Ron McKinney, John Reisinger and Jon Zens objected to the flat lining of Scripture by the Reformed Baptists so that the Law of Moses had greater authority than the law of Christ. Rather, they taught the redemptive-historical timeline of the Bible and a Christ-centered approach to Scripture.

For many years these seven pastors met at conferences, stayed in each other's homes, enjoyed each other's company, and even worked together. For example, Ernie loved to distribute literature for free. Once he decided to offer recent graduates of Southwestern Baptist Theological Seminary a copy of *Abstract of Systematic Theology* by James Pettigru Boyce. Therefore he asked the Seminary for their graduate list so that he and Ron could give everyone a book on the doctrines of grace. Eventually they distributed 20,000 books. One of them ended up in the hands of R. Albert Mohler Jr., a teenager in Florida. Dr. Mohler believed the doctrines of grace as a result of reading that book and became the president of the Southern Baptist Theological Seminary at the age of thirty-two. The Lord used Mohler to help reverse liberalism in the Southern Baptist Convention. Today many young preachers are graduating from Southern and are starting to embrace NCT teaching.

JON ZENS

God used Jon Zens as the catalyst to jumpstart a discussion of law in the new covenant. These discussions eventually led to the NCT movement.

Zens did not have any preconceived ideas to fall back on since he did not come from a Christian home. In 1964, God saved him through an exposition of Galatians at a Fundamentalist Baptist church in Canoga Park, California. Zens soon switched from being a California State Art major to study for the ministry at Bob Jones University, a fervently anti-Calvinistic institution. In 1967, he became convinced of God's initiative in salvation after reading some Calvinistic literature that he found on campus. Therefore he transferred to Covenant College in Lookout Mountain, Georgia, and graduated in 1968. Afterward he enrolled in Westminster Seminary and graduated with a M.Div. in 1972. One of his professors of biblical theology, Meredith Kline, started his thinking about the covenantal discontinuity between the Old and New Testaments.

Zens holds a D.Min. from the California Graduate School of Theology. He published his doctoral thesis in an edited form in

1997 as "'This is My Beloved Son, Hear Him': The Foundation for New Covenant Ethics and Ecclesiology."

Around 1972, he presented two lessons for a Sunday school class at Sovereign Grace Baptist Church in Prospectville, Pennsylvania, entitled, "Covenants and the O.T." and "Covenants in the N.T." He said:

> I fully expected to be thrown out of the church, for I not only rejected the Dispensationalist interpretation which stressed *discontinuity* in God's program, but I also felt compelled to reject the *one 'Covenant of Grace'* (continuity) position of Covenant Theology. I concluded that neither system did justice to the biblical data, and that both systems had to skip over or twist much Scripture in order to sustain their positions (italics Zens').[1]

Instead of upsetting his listeners, he stimulated them into thinking about those issues. Nevertheless he did not think any more about it himself until 1974 when he read an article by E. W. Johnson on "Imputation" in the *Baptist Reformation Review* (*BRR*).[2] Once again, he pondered issues in covenant theology that disturbed him, namely the idea of a covenant of redemption. Zens read in Scripture that the Triune God chose to send Jesus the Son as a sacrifice for sinners before the creation of the world (1 Peter 1: 18–20). He could not, however, find any evidence in the Bible of a covenant between the Father, Son and Holy Spirit, called a covenant of redemption. Therefore Zens agreed with E. W. Johnson and commented on his article in a later *BRR*:[3]

1　Jon Zens, "Law and Ministry in the Church: An Informal Essay On Some Historical Developments (1972–1984)," *Searching Together*, 40, no. 01–04, 40th Anniversary (2014): 17.

2　E. W. Johnson, "Imputation," *Baptist Reformation Review*, (Summer, 1974): 21–45.

3　Jon Zens, "Reflections on E.W. Johnson's 'Imputation' Article" *BRR*, 4:1, 1975, 57–62, 57.

Specifically, however, it should be acknowledged that his point is especially well taken regarding the alleged "covenant of redemption"…As theologians have presented this "covenant of grace," they have simply posited its existence, and have not shown its presence in the Bible. There is an eternal purpose of God in Christ Jesus, and there are historical covenants revealed in Scripture. But a 'covenant of grace' which stands above history does not appear to be a Scriptural concept."[4]

In 1973, Norbert Ward, the editor of the *Baptist Reformation Review*, published an article on Jonathan Edwards by Zens. The following year they met at a Bible Conference in New Jersey. Ward invited Zens to move to Nashville, Tennessee, to become part of a house church, which he did in 1975. Then in 1976, Ward asked Zens to become associate editor of the *BRR*. After Ward suffered a heart attack in December, 1977, he asked Zens to become the editor of the magazine in 1978.

Zens experienced a pivotal change in his thinking in 1977. He had been a guest-speaker that February at New Covenant Baptist Church, in Little Rock, Arkansas. Afterward the elders, David Steele, Curtis Thomas and Theron Howard, asked him to consider the following verses: Ephesians 2:15, Colossians 2:20–23, and 2 Corinthians 3:13–14. They asked Zens to think about the fact that God had removed or abolished the Law. They also challenged him to read Leonard Verduin's *The Reformers & Their Stepchildren*. Upon reading this work, this book had a permanent effect on his thinking. Zens explains:

> On my last day there the three elders asked me some pointed questions about living under grace or law, and they encouraged me to read Leonard Verduin's *The Reformers & Their Stepchildren*. I read this book in June, 1977, and it knocked me off my horse. Soon after this I read Howard Snyder's *The Problem of Wineskins*. My fundamental assumptions about church and the

---

4   Jon Zens, "Law and Ministry in the Church," *Searching Together*, 18.

Christian life were being challenged. I felt compelled to express the burdens that were coming upon my heart. I wrote "Is There A 'Covenant of Grace'?" and it appeared in the Autumn, 1977, *BRR*. This was followed by "Crucial Thoughts Concerning 'Law' in the New Covenant" in the Spring, 1978, *BRR*. These two articles caused quite a stir and became the foundation for developing the implications of the New Commandment for body-life in future writings.[5]

Zens explains why he wrote "Is There A 'Covenant of Grace?'" in his introduction to the article:

With the contemporary rise of interest in Calvinistic theology, the thinking of many Christians has been radically changed. To a good number of brethren, the realization that the essential structure of doctrine they learned for years in evangelical-fundamentalism was defective and anemic has brought about what might be termed "spiritual shock." The bulk of their past cherished assumptions ("free-will," "carnal Christians," the "altar call," the "pre-tribulation rapture," etc.) have had to be scrapped.

In this rebuilding process, not a few Baptists have incorrectly assumed that the only alternative to the Arminian and Dispensational scheme is "Covenant Theology." So they go "all the way" and embrace infant baptism, thinking that a "covenantal" approach to history necessarily involves abandonment of a Baptist position....

However, it seems to me that there is one concept that is consistently *assumed* by many Calvinistic Baptists and all Calvinistic paedobaptists where our thinking needs to be Biblically sharpened. This is the "covenant of grace" concept (italics Zens').[6]

He concludes his article by saying:

---

5   Jon Zens, "A More Gradual Journey Out of the Pastorate," 2, last modified (date), accessed March 21, 2014, http://www.housechurchresource.org/expastors/gradual-zens.html.

6   Jon Zens, "Is There A 'Covenant Of Grace?'", *Baptist Reformation Review*, 6, no. 3, (Autumn 1977): 43.

Using the "one covenant/various administrations" as a rationale to include infants in the church creates tensions which I have yet seen to be dealt with satisfactorily by covenant theologians....

The infants of believers are in some mysterious way both condemned and holy; in Adam and yet in Christ; under wrath and yet a church member. If infants are at birth concretely reckoned as condemned in solidarity with Adam (per Hodge), then what translates them from wrath to grace? Their birth from Christian parents? Their baptism? Certainly not because they have "with the heart believed unto righteousness" (Rom. 10:10)!

...If we stick with the Biblical presentation of one "purpose" in Christ, and a *plurality* of covenants in history, we will avoid the confusion of Dispensationalism's earthly-purpose-for-Israel/heavenly-purpose-for-church theory, and the unnecessary assumptions of Covenant Theology which are used to bring infants into the New Covenant church.[7]

Zens' article "Crucial Thoughts On 'Law' In The New Covenant" continued the discussion. He writes:

I think my point is well-taken within the confines of this specific purpose. The history of Reformed thought reveals a tendency to view the Ten Commandments apart from the progress of redemptive history. I am seeking to point out that "law" in these "last days" is solely in the hands of Christ, not Moses. And in order to establish this point, it is imperative to see that the Mosaic law-covenant was a unified code which had a beginning and end in history. To be sure, the Ten Commandments occupied a special place in the Old Covenant; but this does not detract from the point I made, and wish to now further develop.

3. I am convinced that "law" must always be located in relationship to the advance of redemptive history. The Law of Moses (as a totality) was connected to a particular covenant people. It was codified after a specific act of redemption, the Exodus. In the ratification of this Old Covenant, a nation was constituted and set apart for the Lord.

---

7   Ibid., 51–53.

But in the ultimate purpose of God, this Mosaic economy was *temporary*, destined to exist "until the time of reformation" (Heb. 9:10) when God would speak in a final way in His Son in the last days (Heb. 1:1–2) Everything going on in Israel was of a *typical* nature, and was fulfilled in the person and work of Christ (Heb. 3:5; 8:5; 9:8–9). With the coming of Christ and the ratification of the New Covenant, the Spirit was given to the new Israel—the church. The Old Covenant then passes away in terms of redemptive culmination in the Messiah....

This is simply to say, then, that "law" must now be identified with the current covenant in force, for the former covenant is no longer operative (emphasis Zens').[8]

Later in the article, in dealing with the question of the Sabbath, Zens states:

I have difficulty, therefore, in saying that the Sabbath is universally and perpetually binding on *all men*. It seems rather to be a special ordinance for the covenant people only, just as the Lord's Day has special significance only for Christians....

Christians, then, should be careful about harshly judging one another with regard to observance of the Lord's Day. The stricter "Sabbatarians" should not label Christians who reject the Sabbath principle as "loose" or "antinomian," if these brethren use the Lord's Day in terms of Biblical priorities. And those who do not hold to the "Christian Sabbath" should not label "Sabbatarians" as "legalists," unless these brethren impose their strictness as binding upon the consciences of others (emphasis Zens').[9]

He concludes:

The way the Apostles and prophets used the Old Testament is normative for this age. In light of the person and work of Christ, they interpreted the preparative history before Christ. The

---

8   Jon Zens, "Crucial Thoughts On 'Law' In The New Covenant," *Baptist Reformation Review*, 7, no. 3, (Spring 1978): 10.

9   Ibid., 14.

organic historical connection, and the Christocentric nature that obtains between the Old and New Covenants guarantees the usefulness of the Old Testament for the church; the progression of history to a final New Covenant guarantees the "law of Christ" to be sufficient for the church. The Old Covenant documents constituted "law" for that time period for Israel; the New Covenant documents are binding for the new people of God until the end of this age. Just as Israel had to *anticipate* the future revelation of the Messiah in the New Covenant age, so the church cannot ignore the *past* historic progression toward Christ deposited in the Old Testament. To push Moses' law (as a totality) into the New Covenant is legalism; to take "law" out of the New Covenant is antinomianism; to see redemptive history culminate in Christ Who seals the New Covenant, and as Mediator gives "law" to His servants is Biblical....

I challenge all of you to seriously consider what I have said with an open Bible, for these issues focus on the words of Christ which are most basic to the fabric of the Christian life—"if you love Me, keep My commandments" (John 14:15) (emphasis Zens').[10]

Since Zens had no longstanding loyalty to any particular church and its doctrine, he questioned everything he heard against the Scriptures. Thus Presbyterian & Reformed Publishing Company published his first book, *Dispensationalism: An Inquiry into Its leading Figures and Features*, in 1978. Then his two articles in the *Baptist Reformation Review* caused a great furor among Calvinistic Baptists. Therefore in the late 1970s, Zens found himself at the center of controversy because of those two articles. In the 40th anniversary issue of *Searching Together*, he writes:

In 1978 and 1979 the opposition to the articles in *BRR* accelerated (accompanied also by a number of positive encouragements!). Walt Chantry, a leader among the "Reformed Baptists" in the northeast, wrote a brief letter and accused me (without

10 Ibid., 16, 17.

providing any documentation) of propagating "neo-dispensationalism" and "neo-antinomianism" (July, 1978).

I spent hours at the Vanderbilt Library in Nashville researching "antinomianism," and documented in my lengthy reply to Walt why I repudiated it. I re-sent Walt my articles that disturbed him, and asked him to underline any sentences that bothered him, and told him that I would be glad to consider any points he wished to make (August, 1978). No reply was ever received.[11]

Meanwhile Zens also spent time in the Vanderbilt Library researching law/gospel and Christian ethics. He asked the Lord to guide him in his reading. Soon he discovered A. J. Bandstra's *The Law and the Elements of the World: An Exegetical Study in Aspects of Paul's Teaching* and F. F. Bruce's *Paul: Apostle of the Heart Set Free*. Both of those books encouraged him because he found out others were thinking similar thoughts as him about Christian ethics.

In the winter 1978 issue of *BRR*, Zens published letters on both sides of this issue. A long letter from Don Garlington is an example of one who opposed him:

> The purpose of this letter is not to engage you in a detailed debate concerning your article on the law…Unless it is understood that the law is the factor which placed Israel and the Gentiles in a judicially identical position, then Paul's entire polemic is short-circuited. He presupposes that an equation can be drawn between what Israel possessed in written form and that which the heathen possessed as a law internally written upon their hearts.
>
> When these data are compared with 2 Cor. 3, a remarkable pattern begins to emerge. At the beginning of the human race the law of God was inscribed on the hearts of our first parents. Upon the advent of sin this law of the heart (or conscience)

---

11 Jon Zens, "Law And Ministry in the Church," *Searching Together*, 19.

was defaced and marred, therefore becoming unreliable (in itself) as a guide for belief and conduct. Accordingly, in the giving of the Mosaic ordinances the Lord once again writes this elemental law: this time on tablets of stone. In fact, this very mode of revelation highlights the abiding significance of the decalogue, pointing as it does to the permanence of the ten words....In effect, then, the law written on the heart of the believer in the new covenant constitutes a rewriting of the aboriginal legislation, which under Moses could only command obedience without imparting life, but which under Christ procures for the Christian a reinstatement into the favor of God, a new creation....

In conclusion, let me say that the central issue of this controversy, as I see it, finds expression in that saying of Christ, "Whoever then relaxes one of the least of these commandments and teaches men so, shall be called least in the kingdom of heaven" (Matt. 5:19a)....To be sure, it is a grave error to impose burdens on men which the Lord Himself has not seen fit to impose. However, it is equally iniquitous to subtract from the perceptive will of God and to engender in the people of God an attitude of laxness with regard to any of the commandments.[12]

In the same *BRR* a more sympathetic reader asked Zens to clarify what he meant:

I have just finished reading your article on "Crucial Thoughts Concerning 'Law' in the New Covenant." An excellent article that extends my thinking into areas yet unplumbed. By this article do you mean the following:

1. That we as N.T. Christians are only under what is revealed as the "law of Christ" in the N.T.?

---

12 Don Garlington, Instructor Trinity Ministerial Academy, Essex Fells, New Jersey, [letter to the editor], *Baptist Reformation Review*, 7, no. 4 (Winter 1978): 17–19.

2. That the O.T. law should not be used to alert sinners—rather, we should use the "law of Christ" and Rom. 1 to point out their falling short and condemnation?[13]

Zens replied:

"While he yet spoke, behold, a bright cloud overshadowed them: and behold a voice out of the cloud, which said: 'this is my beloved Son, in whom I am well pleased; hear him'"... (cf. Mark 9:2–9).

In this significant passage two of the most revered Old Testament figures appear with Christ to these three apostles (v.3). Moses the great leader is associated with the giving of the law; Elijah the great prophet is associated with a powerful sign ministry. But Deut. 18:15, 18 is ultimately in view: "the Lord your God will raise up to you a prophet from the midst of you, of your brethren, like unto me; to him you shall hearken." Peter saw this passage fulfilled in the ministry of Christ (Acts 3:22–23). But what is the conspicuous focus which is revealed concerning this final Prophet? It is His *words*: "him you shall hear in all things (cf. Matt. 28:20), whatsoever he shall say to you" (Acts 3:23). The Transfiguration of Christ taught the apostles something epochally significant, namely, that they were to listen to Him as the Prophet God had sent in fulfillment of Deut. 18:15, 18...In order to be obedient to the focus on the words of Christ, must we not likewise find in His teachings the specific norms for our conduct?...

What are faithful ministers of the New Covenant to proclaim? Again, our Saviour who possesses all authority in heaven and earth (28:18) tells us that we have warrant to be blessed in preaching all that He has commanded. This does not mean that we have nothing to do with Moses, but it surely means that we must see Moses as he is viewed in the light of redemptive-historical progress (emphasis Zens').[14]

---

13 Jon Zens, "'This Is My Beloved Son...Hear Him': A Study Of The Development Of Law In The History Of Redemption," *Baptist Reformation Review*, 7, no. 4 (Winter 1978): 15.

14 Ibid., 27.

Later in the article Zens explains:

> Here I wish to simply emphasize the point that *law must be identified with the covenant in force*. We are faced with a delicate balance which must be maintained. In the New Testament, we are confronted with two facts about the Old Testament: (1) the Mosaic covenant administration as a whole has been terminated in history, and succeeded by a better covenant; (2) the Old Covenant documents, however, still remain as valuable and necessary to the New Covenant community. It seems to me that a failure to make this basic distinction has caused confusion, for many would feel that to make the first assertion is tantamount to "throwing out the Old Testament." But such is definitely not the case...(emphasis Zens').[15]

Zens sent a copy of the Winter 1978 *BRR* to a Presbyterian, Dr. Francis Nigel Lee, who responded in a letter:

> I agree with you entirely that the basic difference between us is indeed a *hermeneutical* one!...
>
> As a consistent Baptist, you would answer that all Christian doctrine must be based on the *New* Testament (and not the Old). As a consistent Presbyterian, I would answer that all Christian doctrine must be *based* on the *Old* Testament (*and* developed in the *New*)! You believe that the New Testament is essentially *different* from the Old. I believe that the New Testament is essentially *similar* to the Old. You, in your *hermeneutical* line of Marcionism-Anabaptism-Dispensationalism-Liberalism, root yourself only in the last 27 books of the inerrant Word of God. I, in the *hermeneutical* line of Paul-Augustine-Calvin—Westminster, root myself fully in all 66 books of *all* Scripture which is given by inspiration of God (2 Tim. 3:16). In one word, you are a "New Testament Christian" trying to promote "New Testament Christianity"; whereas I am a "Biblical Christian" trying to promote "Biblical Christianity." Thank God we do have the New Testament in common! How sad, though, that you have *hermeneutically* abandoned the *Old* Testament in which *our Lord Jesus* grounded Himself!...

---

15 Ibid., 34.

I am grateful that, like your correspondent...you too apparently see the need for "Baptists, especially Reformed Baptists," to "begin to move away from...Baptisterianism." I am saddened that you would like to see them "move away" toward an Anabaptist reconstruction of a "New Testament (?!) ethic"...

I could wish the full implications of your departure from Calvinistic Puritanism at these crucial points would cause your more orthodox brethren, Don Garlington...and Walt Chantry...and Charles Spurgeon...with whom you, though a fellow Baptist, are in disagreement, to re-evaluate their own "Baptisterianism"! From my point of view—and yours, too, I would imagine—these dedicated Christian leaders are inconsistent mixtures of Calvinistic Puritanism and remnantal Anabaptism. But no man can (ultimately) keep on adhering to two theologies! In the end, he will be "devoted" to the one and "despise" the other!...But may the ultimate theological development of Garlington and Chantry bring them to *consistent* Calvinism! And may they then win you over...(italics Lee's).[16]

Zens replied to Lee:

I certainly do not believe that every doctrine we embrace must come only from the NT! Obviously, there is doctrinal development from old age to new age. But there is also a shift from many details in the OT to general principles in the NT....

To put me in the line of Marcionism-Liberalism-etc. is ludicrous. I fully accept the inspiration and authority of the OT; but I believe that the progress of redemptive history, and the revelation of the NT, drive us to approach the OT in light of the final speaking of God in Christ.

Mr. Lee is to be commended for seeing the serious problem of "Baptisterianism." To try to mix the Reformed world-view with Baptist tenets is unworkable. As long as Baptists try to hold

---

16 Francis Nigel Lee, [Letter to the editor], *Baptist Reformation Review*, 11, no. 1 (Spring 1982): 19, 20.

their distinctives within the essential framework of Covenant Theology, they will ultimately be frustrated.[17]

How sad a Presbyterian recognized the inconsistencies in the theology of the Reformed Baptists, but the Baptists did not! They only considered Zens' articles militant and divisive.

In January 1979, Zens attended a preacher's fellowship in Dalton, Georgia, where John Reisinger and Ferrell Griswold spoke on the law of God. Zens went with fear and trembling, wondering if he would be shunned, but he was warmly received. Later Zens wrote:

> John's exposition of Galatians 3 and 4 was excellent. He opened his talk by asking how many present read *BRR*—a few hands went up. He then mentioned the significance he felt was attached to my article on the "Covenant of Grace." And commented that my editorial, "What Can We Learn from Reformation History?" "almost made me a Baptist!"[18]

In August 1979, Ted Christman of Covenant Grace Church in Owensboro, Kentucky, sent Zens a letter urging him to recant his position on God's law. Christman wrote:

> Though I do not have time at the present to indicate the reasons why, I must inform you that I am very disappointed in the positions you have taken toward God's law—I'm convinced that it is an over-reaction (as is nearly always the case in church history) to legalistic abuses of the same.
>
> As of yet, you are a relatively young man. I would encourage you to realign yourself with the orthodoxy of the Reformers and the Puritans. This will do at least two things. One, it will maintain your positive influence in the movement which needs you; and two, it will spare you of the retrospective recantations of old age.[19]

---

17 Jon Zens, [Reply to above], Ibid., 20.

18 Jon Zens, "Law And Ministry in the Church," *Searching Together*, 22.

19 Ted Christman, "A Letter From A Concerned Church Leader To Jon Zens (1979)," *Searching Together*, 55, 56.

In December 1979, Zens replied to Christman:

> First, I cannot view what I have written on Law as an "over-reaction." I see it as, rather, a *balancing* attempt to do *justice to Scripture*—which, in crucial areas, neither Dispensationalism nor Covenant Theology have done. My position may seem "extreme" in comparison to certain creedal embodiments; but the issue must be: is a position extreme when compared to a viable opening up of NT texts? I am open to correction *from Scripture*; I have not written a bunch of speculative remarks; I have wrestled with a number of crucial passages, and I believe a *Christ-centered* ethical structure emerges which is lacking in both Dispensationalism and Covenant Theology....
>
> It seems to me that you are confusedly equating "orthodoxy" with a whole system. And I think this is the crux of the matter which you need to reflect upon more carefully: *are the Westminster Confession's statements on church/state, Sabbath/law, Covenant of Works/Covenant of Grace, ecclesiology/infant baptism the essence of a Grace Gospel?* (italics Zens'). [20]

Reflecting on Christman's letter thirty-five years later, Zens wrote:

> Well, Ted is still in Owensboro, KY. The church there now is called Heritage Baptist Church. As the years have rolled on, I guess I'm a relatively older man now! I have not had reason to recant concerning the Christ-centered, New Covenant-based approach that has developed since my first article, "Is There A 'Covenant of Grace'?" that broke the ice in 1977. If anything, the perspectives Ted expressed concern about have only been further solidified with the passing of time and research. In a sense, 1946 can be viewed as a turning-point in New Testament theology. In that year, C. H. Dodd gave his ground-breaking William Ainslie Memorial Lecture, "The Gospel & the Law of

---

20 Jon Zens, [Reply to above], Ibid., 56–59.

Christ."[21] Forty years later Douglas Webster expressed the general consensus of NT scholars:

> The Christian ethic is exclusively dependent upon Christian redemption. . . . Jesus' cross is planted squarely at the center of the believer's existence, providing both the means of salvation and the challenge of a new life-style (*A Passion for Christ: An Evangelical Christology*, Zondervan, 1987, pp.149, 153).

The striking words of God from the cloud, echoing the prophecy of Moses in Deut.18, must ever shape our perspectives in the Gospel age—"This is my Beloved Son, with him I am well-pleased. Listen to him" (Matt.17:5).[22]

Then in 1981, Zens did the typesetting for The First London Confession of Faith (1646) so that Donald Moffit, the head of Backus Books, in Rochester, New York, could publish it. Writing in 1982, Mark McCulley concludes, "The First London Confession is significant for our study in many ways. First, recently reprinted by a modern Particular Baptist publisher, it will probably serve as the basis for a new Sovereign Grace Baptist association if one is formed."[23] The following year the Continental Baptists did form an association of churches founded on the First London Confession of 1644 or 1646.

By 1981, Zens found himself facing another battle front. Those who supported his stand against covenant theology

---

21 C. H. Dodd, *Gospel and Law*, p 64: "The ethical precepts of the Gospels serve two purposes. On the one hand, they help towards an intelligent and realistic act of 'repentance,' because they offer an objective standard of judgment upon our conduct....On the other hand, they are intended to offer positive moral guidance for action, to those who have received the Kingdom of God;" cited by Mark McCulley, *Studies in History and Ethics*, back of front cover.

22 Jon Zens, "A Letter From A Concerned Church Leader To Jon Zens (1979)," *Searching Together*, 61.

23 Mark McCulley, *Studies in History and Ethics*, 12.

disagreed with him on the proper way to "do church." How to conduct church became his passion and led him away from congregational church government to the house church movement. Zens explains his beliefs:

> I personally have come to the conviction that the greatest practical need facing the church today is the recovery of the "*polyform ministry of grace*"...
>
> As *BRR* from 1981 onwards began to assert the obvious disparity between the "polyform" ministry found in the NT and the "ordered system" of various post-apostolic traditions, then even those who agreed with our New Covenant orientation began to be displeased and concerned (italics Zens').[24]

Mark McCulley explains more clearly what Zens means by a polyform ministry:

> Only later, in the Summer, 1981, *BRR* would the controversial assertion of every-member ministry become plain and evident. Zens included 1 Pet. 2:5 on the front cover—"You also, like living stones, are being built into a spiritual house to be a holy priesthood, offering spiritual sacrifices." The emphasis of the *BRR* was obviously no longer soteriological but more ecclesiological, ethical, and practical. After a historical study of Ignatius and Cyprian, "The Rise of One-Bishop Rule in the Early Church" (Judy Schindler), Zens addressed the question directly: "Building Up the Body—One Man or One Another?" Circulated privately among Particular Baptists for a year before its printing (with various reactions of both reservation and reception), this paper faced the single most controversial topic among Particular Baptists...

---

24 Jon Zens, "Law and Ministry in the Church" *Searching Together*, 28. In contrasting a "polyform ministry" with an "ordered system," Zens notes in his article that George Wolfgang Forell made "astute observations about the tragic shift from mutual ministry to unilateral dominion in the early church;" citation from George Wolfgang Forell, *History of Christian Ethics*, I (Minneapolis, MN: Augsburg, 1979), 39.

Being quite practical and specific, Zens denied that elders constitute Christ's authority in the church, and denied that there was any Scriptural warrant to separate one man as "pastor" in distinction from other "elders."[25]

McCulley elaborates on the necessity of a polyform ministry by quoting Zens:

> But how will the Word reign in our gatherings if one man does not do most of the teaching?....We are probably so used to thinking in terms of one man's ministry that *one-anothering* is new to us. Therefore, we must orient ourselves to the fact that the centrality of the Word must not be equated with the speaking of one man. The N.T. nowhere makes that equation (italics Zens').[26]

McCulley comments further:

> Informed by an eschatological perspective of the "other world" to come, Zens called for an "other world" now, one in which the "laity" would be eliminated and all in the covenant would be the "clergy," the "share" or "inheritance" of the Lord (1 Pet. 5:3)....
>
> *BRR* had begun its move toward practicality by listening to all sides; accepting discontinuity with historic Calvinistic theology, it suggested a covenantal discontinuity between Moses and Christ; and seeing the practical and *significant* results of this progress in redemptive history, it now urges the *implementation* of the New Covenant standards for priesthood.
>
> *Having come to see that we are not "under law," but "in law to Christ' (1 Cor. 9:21), we must move on to implement the outworkings of His "new commandment" in our lives and in our churches* (italics McCulley's).[27]

---

25 Mark McCulley, *Studies in History And Ethics*, 32.

26 Jon Zens, *BRR*, X: 2, 1981, 25; cited by Mark McCulley, *Studies in History And Ethics*, 32.

27 Mark McCulley, *Studies In History And Ethics*, 32, 33.

ERNEST AND JOHN REISINGER

In my article, "The Bible's Storyline: How it Affects the Doctrine of Salvation," I stated that Jon Zens was the father of NCT.[28] God definitely used Jon Zens to spearhead this movement. However, as soon as Zens became involved with the house church movement, he lost touch with Gary Long, Ron McKinney and John Reisinger. From my point of view, God used John G. Reisinger to nurture and grow NCT. Since a father teaches and cares for his children long term, I consider Reisinger the earthly father of NCT. Nevertheless, I know now that Zens continued to promote NCT, but I had no knowledge of it.

In the early 1950s, Ernie Reisinger founded Grace Chapel in Carlisle, Pennsylvania, through his zealous witness and desire to win others to Christ. After John Reisinger became convinced of the truths contained in the doctrines of grace, he wanted his brother to embrace them also. Therefore he and Herendeen began to give books to the leaders at Grace Chapel. Walter J. Chantry comments:

> Ernie was not the first of the Carlisle group to understand or agree with these old Protestant teachings that were new to Grace Chapel. While others had their hearts enriched and warmed by these awesome truths, Reisinger for a while fought them in his mind.

> Yet when God opened Ernie's eyes to the Biblical teachings of God's sovereign grace in the salvation of sinners, his zeal to spread these teachings and his desire to study theology more deeply were unsurpassed in the congregation. With a deep and

---

28 Heather A. Kendall, "The Bible's Storyline: How It Affects the Doctrine of Salvation," 64. Unfortunately I did not cite where on the Internet that I got that information. I did find this source: Dennis M. Swanson, "Introduction to New Covenant Theology," 152, last modified (date) accessed March 25, 2014, http://www.tms.edu/tmsj/tmsj18f.pdf.

healthy respect for the creeds of Christendom and for the great theologians of days gone by, Ernie plunged into dogged personal study of classic Christian literature. But he also dispensed the literature to others just as quickly as he devoured it personally. There spread great excitement for the treasure-trove of the writings of the Reformers and the Puritans.[29]

By 1959, Grace Chapel changed its name to Grace Baptist Church and subscribed to the London Baptist Confession of Faith of 1689.

Meanwhile in the 1960s and 1970s, Ernie's brother, John, became involved in a number of church plants in Pennsylvania and New York. He was also a pastor in Canada for nine years. Afterward he returned to the United States and spent ten years as an evangelist, preaching in around forty churches a year. When Ernie started his annual Pastors' Conference in Carlisle in 1966, John brought a carload of pastors from Canada. Soon around twenty-five men attended those conferences. Afterward those Canadian pastors enjoyed fellowship with others at the Harvey Cedars and Seaside Conferences. They also began the family-style Carey Conference in Canada.

John always was an independent thinker. He never could buy Sabbatarianism because he believed the Christian's rest was in Christ. While preaching through Galatians, he began to understand the difference between law and grace. He rejoiced in the fact that believers today are not under law but under grace. Therefore by the late 1970s, John began to preach against the applicability of the moral law. Sadly, the brothers never resolved their differences before Ernie's death in 2004.

---

29 Walter J. Chantry, "Building a New Work," 1, 2, last modified (date), accessed March 25, 2014, http://www.gracebaptistcarlisle.org/e_reisinger_bio.htm.

GARY D. LONG

Gary Long became a believer in January 1962, while stationed in Berlin, Germany, as an officer with the army. In 1964, he embraced the doctrines of grace through the teaching ministry of Pastor Stanley Owen in Columbia, Missouri. Then he took time off active duty to go to seminary from 1965 to 1972. He graduated from Dallas Theological Seminary in 1972 with a Th.D. One of Long's professors was S. Lewis Johnson who taught his students how to interpret Christ in all the Scriptures.

Back in active duty at Fort Hood, Texas, Long began a new work in Copperas Cove, Texas. In January 1975, the army re-stationed him to the Pentagon for two years. He taught at a small work in Sterling, Virginia. During those years Long became friends with Albert Martin, Walter Chantry, and Ernest and John Reisinger. In 1977, Long left active duty and, in 1979, began a writing ministry called Sovereign Grace Ministries of San Antonio, Texas.[30]

From 1974 until 2004, Long hosted an annual sovereign grace doctrinal conference in Salado, Texas. He and John Reisinger, S. Lewis Johnson, Ronald McKinney, Steven Carpenter and others spoke regularly at the Salado Conference. In 1979, Long organized the conference on the theme, "The Grace of God and the Glory of the Cross of Christ." John Reisinger spoke on "The Grace of God and the Role of the Cross in the Fulfillment of the Law of God." Steven Carpenter spoke on "The Grace of God and the Role of the Cross in the Lord's Day." Afterward Long commented on Carpenter's message, "This message set forth a strong biblical basis why the Westminster-Puritan concept of the 'Christian Sabbath' was wrong and, therefore, should

---

30 Gary Long's ministry has never been affiliated with the Reformed and Charismatic Sovereign Grace Ministries of Gaithersburg, Maryland.

be distinguished from the Christian's observance of the 'Lord's Day.'"[31] Reformed Baptists grew disturbed and labelled Reisinger and Carpenter Antinomian.

After seminary, Long pondered some issues bothering him concerning eschatology and also concerning law and the gospel. In the microfilm archives at Southwestern Baptist Theological Seminary he discovered the Appendix to the second edition of the First London Confession of Faith (1646) written by Benjamin Cox, also in 1646. He realized how that Confession was different from the Westminster Confession of Faith (1649) and the Second London Confession of Faith (1689). So much of the 1646 Confession and the Appendix by Cox dealt with Christ. There were serious differences, concerning law and the gospel, between the First London Confession and Cox's writing, on the one hand, and the Westminster Confession of 1649 and the Second London Confession of 1689, on the other. Therefore in 1980, Long published the 1646 edition[32] with the following preface:

> In examination of the Westminster Confession of 1647–1649 (including its Larger and Shorter Catechisms), one will find stress placed upon the law of God summarily comprehended in the Mosaic Decalogue as a rule of life for the believer. Conversely, the stress of the 1646 edition of the First London Confession is upon the New Covenant commands of the law of Christ. In sum, *there is a distinctive New Covenant emphasis concerning biblical law in the 1644 and 1646 editions of the First London*

---

31 Gary D. Long, "The Christian Sabbath—Lord's Day Controversy," 3: footnote 3, last modified (date) accessed January 29, 2015, http://www.ptsco.org/The Christian Sabbath booklet.pdf.

32 Gary D. Long republished *The First London Confession of Faith 1646 Edition* with the Appendix by Benjamin Cox in 1985 and in 2004 in order to highlight the differences between it and other Baptist Confessions of Faith. *The First London Confession of Faith, 1646 Edition* (Belton, TX: Sovereign Grace Ministries, 2004).

Confession that is distinctly lacking in the Old Covenant empha-
sis of the Westminster and 1689 London Confessions (emphasis
Long's).[33]

By the late 1970s, Reformed Baptists and Sovereign Grace
Baptists divided over the issue of the Sabbath. The Reformed
Baptists insisted that the command to keep the Sabbath applied
to Christians because it was part of the moral everlasting law of
God. Sovereign Baptists, on the other hand, viewed the Lord's
Day as a special day under the new covenant. Long explains how
the disagreement between the two escalated over time:

> And so, in the late 1970s differences arose *within* the
> Reformed Baptists, especially over the Sabbath and its being
> eternal *moral* law. (*Reformed* Baptists is a title that has to be
> explained as referring primarily to *soteriological Calvinism* not
> *ecclesiological Calvinism*;...) The differences began to result in
> some *Reformed Baptists* teaching that the Sabbath command-
> ment was eternal moral law, most of whom preferred the 1689
> London Confession and others (including myself) who did
> not, who began to be called *Sovereign Grace Baptists* preferring
> the 1646 London Confession. Charges of Antinomianism
> (against law) from some Reformed Baptists who held to the
> 1689 Confession began to be directed at some of us who did
> not agree with their understanding of the covenantal system of
> Reformed Theology and its teaching of one overarching cov-
> enant of grace. The charges were especially directed against
> John Reisinger in his writings (in *The Sword and Trowel* maga-
> zine later called *Sound of Grace*) and evangelistic preaching,
> which included messages he delivered at the end of the 1970s
> at the Salado Conference. In February 1980, to help defend
> John from what I believed to be unjust charges, I published a
> doctrinal pamphlet entitled, *The Christian Sabbath Lord's Day*

---

33 Gary D. Long, 1980 Preface to *The First London Confession of Faith 1646
   Edition*, viii.

Controversy, teaching that the Sabbath was not a creation ordinance (italics Long's).[34]

In the preface, Long states:

This pamphlet on the "Christian Sabbath-Lord's Day" issue has been written in a pastoral manner to stimulate a biblical solution to a doctrinal controversy that currently exists among Reformed Baptists. The author believes reconciliation is possible between those who differ within the Reformed Baptist movement, but only by their first agreeing upon a biblical method of interpretation developed from a study of the New Testament use of the Old while keeping in mind the God-centered covenantal settings of both the Old and New Covenants with their Christ-centered emphasis. He also believes that there needs to be an in-depth look at church history and study of historical theology with a special emphasis placed upon the theological lineage of the believers-church concept of the Swiss Brethren and the early English Particular Baptists and New England Baptists....

Having written the pamphlet the author realizes that many have called themselves "Reformed Baptists" in the past because of their belief in "the doctrines of grace," not because of the "Reformed Faith" doctrine of the church, namely, belief in infant baptism and a non-confessing church membership by those who are "outwardly" in "the covenant of grace." But when the doctrine of salvation and the church is combined, the two terms, "Reformed" and "Baptist" are neither biblically nor historically compatible. Therefore, it may be better to make the distinction of "Reformed Baptists" and "Sovereign Grace Baptists."[35]

Long concludes:

The problem presently at hand is this: one side believes that the "Christian Sabbath" hermeneutic will, if consistently carried

---

34 Gary D. Long, "New Covenant Theology: What It Is and How It Differs from Covenant Theology," 15, last modified (date), accessed November 2, 2015, http://gospelpedlar.com/articles/Bible/n_c_theology/NCT-What-It.pdf.

35 Gary D. Long, "The Christian Sabbath—Lord's Day Controversy," 2.

out, lead to a paeodobaptist concept of the Church (both are agreed that this concept of the Church is fundamentally unbiblical). The other side believes that a "Lord's Day" hermeneutic without the fourth commandment will lead to "antinomianism" by unlawfully severing the biblical relationship between the law and the gospel (and, again, both are agreed that this is wholly unbiblical). Which is right? The Scriptures and time will tell. Should this alternative be pursued and, humanly speaking, it probably will be, due to the strong theological convictions involved on both sides, perhaps it would be helpful, while the controversy is *being biblically resolved, to refer to those who hold to the "Christian Sabbath" theology as "Reformed Baptists" and* to those who hold to the "Lord's Day" theology as "Sovereign Grace Baptists." Such a distinction might prove to be a wise interim approach until such time that the issues involved can be finally settled by a Spirit-enabled under-standing of the Scripture determined through consistent, biblical exegesis. *Without an agreed upon biblical hermeneutic to start from, a final solution will never be reached.* I am personally of the opinion that a biblical hermeneutic needs to be developed from the study of the NT use of the OT, keeping in mind the God-centered covenantal settings of both the Old and New Covenants with their Christ-centered emphasis (Luke 24:25-27, 44-48; John 5:46: Acts 13:33; Gal. 6:14)....It was with this conviction in mind that I was prompted to write this pastoral pamphlet. May it serve as a contribution to that end (italics Long's).[36]

Then in 1982, Long chaired a theological committee at a Council on Baptist Theology in Chicago. He presented for adoption *The First London Baptist Confession of Faith, 1646 Edition*; those present gladly accepted his motion.

RONALD W. MCKINNEY

In 1967, Ron McKinney graduated from Bellhaven University in Jackson, Mississippi, with a Bachelor of Arts. He held majors

---

36 Ibid., 23, 24.

in Business and Art and a minor in Bible and Greek. In 1974, he received a M.Div. from Reformed Theological Seminary in Clinton, Mississippi. Then he received his D.Min. from the North American School of Theology in 1990.

Ron McKinney's father, Don, preached for seventy years until three or four weeks before his death. He loved the Word of God and could quote the Old Testament references found in the New Testament. Like John Reisinger, Don never could hold to Sabbatarianism. Ron came to Christ by studying the book of John with his father. He soon saw election in the Scriptures.

After John Reisinger suffered in an automobile accident in 1976, Ron McKinney took over as senior editor of *The Sword and Trowel*. In 1977, Ron moved to Dallas, Texas, to pastor a church. He also continued as senior editor of *The Sword and Trowel*. This paper had a wide international readership as long as Reisinger and McKinney wrote about the doctrines of grace. Near the end it had 28,000 subscriptions in the US and forty-six foreign countries. Yet, when the paper started promoting NCT, the readership quickly dropped off. Since not enough readers supported the paper financially, the board decided to stop publishing the paper by 1987. Ron McKinney did continue publishing *The Sword and Trowel* occasionally, but it became more of a church newsletter. Through the years McKinney has published more than 800 articles and essays.

In 1979, Ron and his close friend Thom Smith struggled with the articles that Jon Zens had written in the *BRR*. Both men were Reformed Baptist pastors committed to the London Baptist Confession of 1689. Yet Smith was seriously thinking of becoming a Presbyterian until two factors changed his mind: a letter from Jon Zens and a plane trip with John Reisinger. In October 1978, Zens had sensed Smith's cold attitude toward him at the Banner of Truth Conference in Atlanta, Georgia. Therefore he wrote him a letter in early 1979. That April Smith called Zens to apologize for giving him the "cold shoulder" at the conference. He also admitted that Zens' articles possibly opened the way for a consistent "Baptist Theology."[37]

Meanwhile Thom Smith and John Reisinger met while flying from Pennsylvania to Oklahoma. Smith was about to become a paedobaptist until John used Galatians 3 to change his mind. Jon Zens told me: "In a strange stroke of Providence, it was because of the partial nuclear meltdown that happened at Three Mile Island, Pennsylvania, on March 28, 1979, that John and Thom ended up on the same plane."[38]

McKinney wanted to discuss the various views on the law at a Banner of Truth Conference. Thomas Chantry and David Dykstra state:

> In 1979, at the second US Banner of Truth conference, McKinney asked Iain Murray and Ernie Reisinger (by that time a trustee of the Banner) if Banner would be willing to invite speakers from across the spectrum to address various views on the law. Murray and Reisinger of course declined; Banner of Truth is governed by a confessional standard (Westminster) and does not exist to promote debate among divergent theologies. Disappointed, McKinney instead hosted a conference called the Council on Baptist Theology in 1980 and 1981.[39]

After the Banner of Truth Conference, McKinney was disappointed other Reformed Baptists would not discuss anything contrary to the Westminster Confession. Therefore he called a meeting at his church in Plano, Texas, to pray and to study Galatians. Four other men attended that meeting in October

---

37 Jon Zens, "Law and Ministry in the Church," *Searching Together*, 21.

38 Jon Zens, e-mail message, March 20, 2015.

39 Thomas Chantry and David Dykstra, *Holding Communion Together*, 72.

1979: his father Don, John Reisinger, Charles Sild, an elder at Ron's church, and Thom Smith. Ron knew his father and John did not believe the Sabbath was an eternal moral law. Ron, however, had been preaching on law from a Reformed Baptist position. Therefore he was glad that an elder from his church and Thom Smith would be at the meeting. By the end of the meeting, those five men reached an understanding of the issues involved. They agreed a conference would be beneficial to discuss these matters with other pastors.

Ron McKinney and the board of directors for *The Sword and Trowel* decided to host a Council on Baptist Theology in 1980 and 1981 called the Dallas Conferences. He also hosted a third conference in 1982 in Plano, Texas, a suburb of Dallas. McKinney issued an invitation in *The Sword and Trowel* and sent out flyers for the first conference to 600 pastors.

The first two conferences were held at the Dupont Plaza Hotel in Dallas; the third at the North Dallas Holiday Inn. These conferences were well-attended and edifying. Discussion was encouraged. For the first time, pastors talked openly about law and grace. The speakers at the first conference were Ron and Don McKinney, John Reisinger, Charles Sild, William Franklin, Jerry Locher, Thom Smith, Gary Scott, Gary Long, Steven Carpenter and Jon Zens. Ron McKinney spoke on "The Doctrine of Adoption;" Jon Zens on "An Examination of the Presuppositions of Covenant and Dispensational Theology;"[40] Steven Carpenter on "Sabbatarianism;" and Gary Scott presented a paper on "Acts and the Use of the Law." Ron McKinney introduced his topic of adoption in this way:

> When the apostle John exclaimed, "Behold, what manner of love the Father hath bestowed [lavished] on us, that we should

---

40 Jon Zens, Law and Ministry in the Church," *Searching Together*, 24.

be called the Sons of God," he was exuberant with the great privilege and blessing of Adoption. To be brought from an alien family and placed into the family of God is the highest privilege to be enjoyed in this life.

The doctrine of Adoption, although a major New Testament theme, has been given a very small place in the development of the creeds and confessions of the Church. It is strange to me that a doctrine so profound in its practical implications and benefits would and could be neglected....Because they failed to see this truth, elements of legalism were bound to appear in their thinking, preaching, and practice.[41]

He continued by saying:

The Galatians were *sons* who were living as slaves in bondage, still under the old covenant law.

We must come to appreciate what it means to be a "son," what it means to not be "under law" but under grace. To be under law means to put the law [in any sense] between my conscience and God whereby my relationship to God is either earned or maintained by my fulfilling the law's requirements....

We have received the "Spirit of Adoption" whereby we cry, "Abba Father." We are no longer slaves but sons....

When we, repent and believe, what place does adoption have in that embrace of faith? John states in his epistle that adoption is the first and greatest privilege that comes to those who believe. We are not just pardoned or accepted but we are given the right [exousia, not dunamis] and authority to be the Sons of God. John is saying that in the initial application of salvation, adoption is foremost and central.

So in the application of salvation the privileges and blessings of the *New Covenant* are immediately realized. We become full-grown sons of God in the family of God.

---

41 Ronald W. McKinney, "Adoption: The Crowning Blessing of the New Covenant," 1. Unpublished paper. n.d.

In the old covenant, even believers were kept in a period of tutorage [i.e. they were in a stage of infancy]. But now, when we embrace the Savior we come into the Kingdom as full-grown mature sons with all the privileges of adoption.

So you see the importance of this doctrine is underscored by John. For in the initial stages of application we become immediately the sons of God. "Now ye are all the children of God by faith in Christ Jesus."

So great is this privilege that only the God who gives it can enable us to *understand* it and attest to the *reality* of it....

Because God has placed you in the position of sons, he has granted you the Spirit of sonship so that you might be enabled to *know and enjoy the privileges of* what he has made you. Without the Holy Spirit we can neither *fathom nor enjoy* that great blessing. It is too far beyond us....The Holy Spirit is given to illuminate our minds of that great privilege. To actually condition our hearts to enjoy it and approach God in the full awareness of it (emphasis McKinney's).[42]

Jon Zens rejoiced to see so many pastors discussing and wrestling with the issues that he had raised in the *BRR*. He brought copies of "'As I Have Loved You': The Starting Point of Christian Obedience," to the conference, which people gladly received. In 1981, he published this article and his plenary talk, "An Examination of the Presuppositions of Covenant and Dispensational Theology," in a book, *Studies in Theology & Ethics*.[43] This book also contained Zens' review of *God's Righteous Kingdom* by Walter Chantry.

Gary Long presented a paper at the 1980 conference entitled, "Biblical Law and Ethics: Absolute and Covenantal." Soon afterward Zens published this paper as a book through the *BRR*. Then

---

42 Ibid., 4, 12, 13.
43 Jon Zens, *Studies in Theology and Ethics* (Malin, OR: BREM, 1981).

in 2008, New Covenant Media republished this work because of the importance of understanding the issues surrounding the controversy between law and grace.

In the 1980 preface Long states:

> This study entitled "Biblical Law and Ethics" is an exegetical polemic for understanding the absolute and covenantal nature of God's law. It has special application to the current controversy on-going within and among those who are Reformed Baptists, but it also addresses the present controversy among Reformed Paedobaptists due to the rise of the "Theonomy Movement."...
>
> Without apology, it is asserted that biblical exegesis and historical theology prove and support the thesis of this study, namely, that Biblical Law has absolute and covenantal distinctives. Therefore, failure to contextually interpret the absolute and covenantal distinctives of biblical law will only prolong the differences that continue to exist within Reformed Theology, whether it be among Reformed Paedobaptists or Reformed Baptists...God forbid that any involved in the present doctrinal controversy should glory "except in the cross of our Lord Jesus Christ."[44]

Furthermore Long explains the absolute and covenantal distinctives of God's laws:

> To use the law of God lawfully, negatively forbids two things and positively recognizes another. First, it forbids making the covenant law of Moses binding upon the New Covenant believer; second, from being unrelated to the law of God, for he is in-lawed to Christ. Why is this so? Because that is what the sacred text contextually says! But a right use of the law recognizes that the believer is *in-lawed* to Christ....And, dear brethren, to be in-lawed to Christ, demands each and all who are led by the indwelling Spirit to recognize and heed that

---

44 Gary D. Long, *Biblical Law and Ethics: Absolute and Covenantal* (Charleston, SC: www.CreateSpace.com, 2014), iii, iv.

ye have been called unto liberty; only use not liberty for an occasion to the flesh, but by love serve one another. For all the law is fulfilled in one word, even in this; Thou shalt love thy neighbour as thyself.... (Gal. 5:13–14...) (italics Long's).[45]

He concludes by emphasizing the meaning of the absolute law of God:

> The covenant law of the New Testament canon written by the Spirit of God upon the tablet of the believing heart is permanent and binding under the New Covenant administration (Jer, 31:31–34; Heb. 8:8–12) of God's eternal purpose (Eph. 3:11). It is revealed in the New Testament gospel of Christ and includes God's unchanging standard of righteousness revealed as *absolute law* in the Old Testament canon and brought to its full eschatological realization in the Messianic mission of Christ (Matt. 5:17–20). Under the New Covenant, the law of Christ (I Cor. 9:20–21) is the "royal law" (Jas. 2:8), the gospel rule, by which the believer, led by the Spirit, is to walk by faith in the Son of God, who loved him, and gave Himself for him (Gal. 2:20) (italics Long's).[46]

In the 2007 preface, Long says he never used the words "New Covenant Theology" in 1980 or in this republished book. He comments:

> The reason it never occurs is because, as a theological system, New Covenant Theology was then only in the early stages of distinguishing itself from those among Reformed Baptists who fully subscribe confessionally to the 1689 London Baptist Confession and its teaching on the law of God which is in agreement with Reformed Paedobaptist Theology and the Westminster Confession of Faith of 1647.[47]

After the 1981 Council on Baptist Theology, some pastors wanted to form an association. They decided to hold a planning

---

45 Ibid., 83, 84.

46 Ibid., 91.

47 Ibid., i.

meeting in November in Plano, Texas, at Ron McKinney's church. Ron McKinney and John Armstrong both felt the need for an association in order to grow. Jon Zens, on the other hand, felt those pastors only wanted "to be something."[48]

Thom Smith asked Zens to meet with several men the evening after Armstrong's presentation. Zens explains:

> In this meeting with eight men, Thom opened by expressing appreciation for the help *BRR* had been in the law/gospel discussion, but felt that the "body-life" teaching found in the magazine was not in line with Baptist tradition, and was causing division in some churches. Seven of the eight men then proceeded to express their reservations, and give alleged examples of where *BRR* articles had caused problems in churches.[49]

WALTER CHANTRY AND AL MARTIN

In the early 1970s, the Reformed Baptist Association consisted of seven churches in the northeastern United States. Walt Chantry's church in Carlisle, Pennsylvania, began sponsoring family conferences at Harvey Cedars in New Jersey. Al Martin and Walter Chantry became the two leading figures for the Reformed Baptists. Both men were quite upset at the writings of Jon Zens and John Reisinger. Moreover they did not approve of Reisinger's presentation on law at the Salado Conference in 1979. Therefore at the Harvey Cedars Conference in June 1979, Walt Chantry preached a series of four lectures on "The Kingdom of God." Thomas Chantry and David Dykstra explain, "In the sermons he [Chantry] sought to distinguish the Reformed view of the Kingdom both from the Theonomic and New Covenant views.

---

48 Jon Zens, "Law and Ministry in the Church," *Searching Together*, 31, 32.
49 Ibid., 32.

Montville's Trinity Pulpit distributed these sermons widely, bringing a response from Jon Zens."[50]

After Jon Zens had listened to the tapes of Chantry from the Harvey Cedars Conference, he found out that Chantry intended to publish those sermons from the conference in a book. He begged Chantry in August 1979 not to print such "flagrant misrepresentations".[51] In September 1979, Chantry wrote Zens a letter:

> It is clear that some major shifts have been made. And your new categories have sown confusion in our churches—not about what we shall call Biblical teachings. Your writings have provoked a new revolt against the very Biblical idea of righteousness and altered the Biblical understanding of the gospel...What has been put into print has been damaging to the cause of Christ...
>
> With complete distaste for controversy, but with greater aversion to your dangerous and confusing novelties,—Walter J. Chantry, Pastor.[52]

Zens and Chantry disagreed on whether or not God intended for the Ten Commandments to be his abiding moral law; as such believers should keep the Sabbath. But Chantry refused to accept Zens' point of view. Therefore Banner of Truth published Chantry's book, *God's Righteous Kingdom: The Law's Connection with the Gospel,* in 1980. Afterward Zens wrote a review. He concludes his review by saying:

> It is sad that Mr. Chantry has spent so much time attacking positions that the "two sides" (whoever they are) do not believe. He has not accurately identified the two extremes he is concerned

---

50 Thomas Chantry and David Dykstra, *Holding Communion Together*, 74.

51 Jon Zens, "A Review Article of Walter Chantry's *God's Righteous Kingdom: The Law's Connection with the Gospel*," 1, last modified (date), accessed March 31, 2014, http://solochristo.com/theology/nct/zens-chantry.htm.

52 Walter J. Chantry, personal letter to Jon Zens, "Law and Ministry in the Church," *Searching Together*, 23.

to refute, and therefore he fails to come to grips with the real issues raised by those who dissent from his opinion. I believe Mr. Chantry's position does not face the redemptive-historical shift from Moses to Christ, from Egyptian exodus to Christ's exodus, which shapes the NT approach to ethics....

Mr. Chantry discourages people from studying the two extremes, which he regards as "counterfeits" (p. 12). But I believe that if they are examined forthrightly, it will be apparent that this book fails to face the specific issues raised by them, and that it does not measure up to "the true currency of heaven" (p. 12).

One does not have to hold to Pastor Chantry's form of narrow nomianism in order to maintain that God's kingdom is righteous. And it appears that an increasing number of believers are raising serious questions that rightly challenge the traditional answers given historically by the systems of Dispensationalism and Covenant Theology. Our Christ-centered Scriptures will give us the answers we need.[53]

In February 1980, Martin preached similar thoughts as Chantry at a pastor's conference in Toronto, Canada. He entitled his highly emotional sermon, "Law and Gospel." Not everyone who heard Martin preach agreed with him, however. James Shantz, a Toronto Baptist Seminary graduate, wrote him a letter saying, "I continue to be greatly dismayed by your lecture on Law and Grace, as I have continued to study it on tape. Your declaration that *BRR*...is teaching antinomianism reveals that you yourself have not carefully studied all the materials."[54]

By 1981, those who espoused NCT were eager to sit down and discuss the issues with those who opposed them. Jon Zens explains what happened:

---

53 Jon Zens, "A Review Article of Walter Chantry's *God's Righteous Kingdom*," 9, 10.

54 Jon Zens, "Law and Ministry in the Church," *Searching Together*, 27.

I think it is important to underscore that in 1981, on two independent occasions, attempts were made to get both sides together and seek more understanding. But in both occasions these attempts were aborted by Walt, Al and Ernie refusing to attend. The first attempt was made by James McColl in connection with the Sovereign Grace Conference in Seaside Heights, New Jersey. When the controversy heightened, James reached out to get both sides together. The NCT parties were willing, the others were not. Then Gary W. Long in Springfield, Missouri, was grieved about the situation. He called me and said that the Sovereign Grace Baptist Church was willing to pay all expenses for six of us, three from each side, to come and have a discussion in Springfield, MO. Again, the three non-NCT persons refused this gracious invitation. Note: neither Gary W. Long nor James McColl knew of the other's efforts to encourage discussion.[55]

Then in 1982, John Reisinger published *The Law/Grace Controversy: A Defense of the Sword and Trowel and the Council on Baptist Theology*. He explains:

"...Love worketh no ill to his neighbor; therefore love is the fulfilling of the law." Romans 13:10

1. I want to defend *The Sword & Trowel*, the men and churches responsible for the Council on Baptist Theology in Dallas in 1980, and 1981, and myself from any false ideas about what we believe and preach. We are not interested in defending our "persons," but we are zealous to defend the truth which has changed our lives and our ministries.

2. I want to put into print what we really believe so that any sincere person can read and judge for himself if our doctrine is according to God's word...

We have pleaded for an open discussion of sections of the Westminster and Philadelphia Confessions of Faith on the

---

55 Jon Zens, e-mail message, March 20, 2015. Please note that this is a different Gary Long from the one who hosted the Salado Conferences in Texas.

basis of the texts of Scripture used to "prove" they were Biblical. All such efforts have been stoutly rejected. The moment we dare not question any group, creed, or individual, but must accept their pronouncements as "absolute truth," we are back into Roman Catholic popery…When we "quote the confession" as if that forever settles the point of discussion, we have lost the Bible as our final and sole authority. We have then replaced the Word of God as our authority with an "official interpretation" of the Word of God as our *real and practical* authority…

It was quite a shock to me when I learned that the Westminster Confession of Faith was formulated and sent to parliament *without any textual references*. The Scripture "proof texts" were added later.…

…When a person or church speaks of their being a "confessional" church, in the sense that it is used historically, they are totally dishonest if they call themselves "Baptist." The fact that the Westminster Confession of Faith says something is sufficient grounds for a Presbyterian to believe it. In fact, he *must* believe it to be a Presbyterian. However, Baptists have never been a "creedal" church in this sense (italics Reisinger's).[56]

Later in the book, Reisinger continues with a discussion on law:

"Everyone who sins breaks the law; in fact, sin is lawlessness." I John 3:4

Sin is not just breaking the ten commandments; it is a basic attitude of self will and anti-authority. "Sin is lawlessness"— PERIOD! Sin is "going our own way" as opposed to God's way. Paul says, "Love fulfills whatever law there is", and John says, "Sin will disobey whatever law there is." Sin is anti-law.…

---

56 John G. Reisinger, *The Law/Grace Controversy: A Defense of the Sword & Trowel and the Council on Baptist Theology* (Berryville, VA: Grace Abounding Ministries, 1982), 1–3.

"This is love for God: to obey his commands. And his commands ARE NOT BURDENSOME." I John 5:3

...The non-Christian loves self and hates law. He lives by one law, "I want to please myself." He gets angry when he is reminded that his behavior is contrary to the law of his Creator and Judge. The Christian's attitude is the exact opposite. God's law is not a burden but a delight. The real grief to God's true sheep is not the strictness of God's law but our inability to obey our Father's will perfectly....

I want to emphasize one more thing from I John 5:3. What does it mean to "love God"? It means "obeying His commands." What could possibly be clearer? How could any person ever read that verse and then try to separate law and love?...The fruit of love is always obedience! And obedience is always to the *will of God* revealed in Scripture, not some imaginary idea that comes out of my emotions (emphasis Reisinger's).[57]

Reisinger concludes by writing:

I hope every reader is totally convinced that the desire of our hearts and the goal of our preaching is to see people living holy lives. We sincerely believe that all of our Reformed Baptist brethren share that same goal....

Obviously how we understand the place and use of the Ten Commandments in the New Testament Scriptures is going to greatly influence both the content and method of our preaching. We can see why there is such a disagreement among Reformed Baptists in how we are to preach to both sinners and saints. If we believe that nothing can fill the heart with love to God except "the preaching of the cross," then obviously the Person and Work of Christ is going to be our major subject and theme in preaching. On the other hand, if we believe that there is an essential "preparation" in a sinner's heart that *only* the preaching of the Ten Commandments can produce, then the tables

---

57 Ibid., 6, 7.

of stone will, of necessity, be the major theme in our preaching (italics Reisinger's).[58]

CALVINISTIC BAPTISTS BY THE MID-1980S

According to Dennis M. Swanson, director of the Master's Seminary Library, Jon Zens is the one who coined the phrase "New Covenant Theology" in 1981.[59] Swanson came to this conclusion by quoting something Zens wrote, "[I]t is my prayer that we will seek only the glory of Christ as we work towards a New Covenant Theology."[60] John Reisinger also used the words "new covenant theology" at the first John Bunyan Conference held in 1981. He said, "I believe it is time to take some positive steps to deliberately make known new covenant theology more effectively and on a wider scale."[61] Then in 1983, John Reisinger preached on NCT at a Salado Conference, hosted by Gary Long. By the mid-1980s, many people described this movement as new covenant theology (NCT).

The friends John Reisinger, Gary Long and Ron McKinney stood for this fledgling new movement called NCT with a belief in the redemptive-historical shift from Moses to Christ. As such they preferred the First London Baptist Confession of Faith of 1644 or 1646 which exalted the Lord Jesus Christ as Prophet, Priest and King. Jon Zens continued to teach NCT but remained estranged from the others because of his developing emphasis on body-life ministry and his rejection of one paid pastor overseeing the flock in the local church.

---

58 Ibid., 22, 23.

59 Dennis M. Swanson, "Introduction to New Covenant Theology," 153.

60 Jon Zens, *Studies in Theology and Ethics*, 1; cited by Dennis Swanson, "Introduction to New Covenant Theology," 153.

61 John G. Reisinger, "When should a Christian Leave a Church?", 16.

Meanwhile Ernie Reisinger, Walt Chantry and Al Martin remained firm with covenant theology on the covenant of grace and two administrations theology of the Westminster Confession. They also continued to believe in the tripartite division of the law into moral, civil and ceremonial commands. As a result the Sabbath was part of the abiding moral law of God.

In June 1983, about twenty Calvinistic Baptist churches in the United States organized into an association holding to NCT and called themselves the Continental Baptists. They believed in the doctrines of grace, autonomous local churches consisting only of believers, and baptism by immersion as a prerequisite to church membership and participation at communion. These Baptists accepted the London Baptist Confession of Faith (1646).

Trinity Baptist Church, in Wheaton, Illinois, where John H. Armstrong was the pastor, hosted the First General Assembly of Continental Baptist Churches. Ronald W. McKinney was the keynote speaker. According to the May/June issue of *The Sword & Trowel*, the following men would participate: Frank Boydstun from Oklahoma, John H. Armstrong from Illinois, David Surpless from Puerto Rico, Edward Collison from Florida, John G. Reisinger from New York, Jerry Locher from Michigan, Donald A. Carson from Illinois, Peter Masters from England, Thomas N. Smith from Oklahoma, Gary L. Scott from Georgia, and Alfred C. Blackwell from New York. I find it interesting that Armstrong invited Surpless from Puerto Rico to talk about missions and Masters from England to lead in one time of worship. An important part of the program included the necessity of drawing up a constitution for legal purposes.

Larry McCall writes:

The Continental Baptist Churches arose from those meetings in Dallas. This was an attempt to unite Baptist churches of like-mindedness on the issues of NCT. As a young pastor...I attended those meetings with great hope. Sadly, within 10 years that association was down to a handful of churches due to differences of philosophy of associations rather than differences over NCT.[62]

Tragically, not everyone who first embraced NCT remained faithful to its claims of truth. Thom Smith converted to the Episcopalian Church; John Armstrong changed into an ecumenical Catholic. Others also fell away—even to this present day.

---

62 Larry McCall, e-mail message, August 13, 2014.

CHAPTER 6

SPREADING THROUGHOUT THE UNITED STATES

When Dr. Berry, a chiropractor, witnessed to the Scaylers, he had no idea how God would use the three of them for his glory. Because of their encouragement John Reisinger started to host the John Bunyan Conference. As a result of this conference and Reisinger's writing ministry, many people grew in their understanding of NCT. But by 2000, opposition from covenant theologians was mounting to NCT. In 2001, Richard Barcellos wrote a book, *In Defense of the Decalogue*, denouncing NCT. In 2002, Tom Wells and Fred Zaspel answered Barcellos in their book, *New Covenant Theology*. By 2007, Gary Long had established a seminary to teach NCT. Meanwhile Jon Zens held his own conferences, Searching Together. Geoff Volker first heard about NCT through the *Baptist Reformation Review* and subsequently met Jon Zens. Geoff Volker now has a worldwide ministry. Thanks to Reisinger's encouragement of a younger pastor, A. Blake White became influential in the NCT movement through his books.

LLOYD AND JUDITH SCAYLER

Lloyd Scalyer was born and raised according to Jewish tradition. In 1968, he and his wife Judith left New York City to settle in

Ronks, near Lancaster, Pennsylvania. They bought some property and built a motel there. While the motel underwent construction, Lloyd suffered from a painful back. Therefore he visited Dr. Thomas Berry, a chiropractor, in nearby Strasburg. Dr. Berry asked him if he had given consideration to the claims of Christ on his life. He answered, "I am Jewish, and I am not interested in Jesus." Lloyd writes in his testimony, "I couldn't believe it! This guy must be nuts! Can you imagine asking me, someone who is Jewish, if I ever gave adult consideration to the claims of Christ on my life? Because of Jesus, my people were persecuted, suffered, and died. He could never be the long awaited Messiah!"[1] Nevertheless while reading the Old Testament, God soon saved him.

Lloyd and Judith first met John Reisinger around 1972 when they were missionaries to the Jews with Emmanuel's Mission. Then in the fall of 1979, they heard John preach on law and grace at the Seaside Heights Conference in New Jersey. Now this was a difficult issue whenever they witnessed to other Jews. Since the Scaylers wanted to talk to John more about law and grace, and to get his advice, they invited him and his wife Rosie to dinner.

That evening Judith asked, "John, why don't we have a conference ourselves to deal strictly with the issue of law and grace?" After discussing it with John, the Scaylers offered to hold the conference in their motel and to do it in the spring of 1980. Therefore that spring the Scaylers, John Reisinger, and Dr. Thomas Berry met in the Scayler's living room. Dr. Berry suggested calling the conference the John Bunyan Conference; for John Bunyan (1628–1688) had written an article on the

---

1   Lloyd Elias Scalyer, "It was there all the time…," 1, Unpublished pamphlet, n.d.

relationship of Moses' Law to the Christian—the same issue confronting the church today.

THE JOHN BUNYAN CONFERENCE

In 1981, John Reisinger held the first official John Bunyan Conference in Lancaster, Pennsylvania, with fifty people in attendance. They stayed in the Scaylors' motel and held the conference in the fire hall. The subject of the conference was on law and grace, and his first message was entitled, "John Bunyan and the Law."

Reisinger found that many of his listeners had recently been forced to leave churches with "a heavy 'law ministry' where the Elders were the 'Lords and Masters' of the Assembly."[2] Such pastors did not allow believers to experience the joy of their salvation; for they continually dragged them back to Moses and the Ten Commandments. They also did not allow them to think for themselves. Disagreement with a pastor was not allowed. "The hallowed creed produced by our 'Godly inspired forefathers' became a sword to silence anyone daring to ask a question. The creed and the pastor's personal power became the final authority over the church and the conscience of the individual."[3] Although disagreeing with Walter Chantry on the function of the Mosaic Law in salvation and sanctification, Reisinger agreed wholeheartedly with him on the issue of tyrannical pastors. He quoted Chantry:

> Arrogance and an overbearing spirit is never acceptable in elders. Popish demeanor reveals pride in the heart. Pompous and tyrannical treatment of subordinates almost universally attends positions of authority in the world and in human

---

2   John G. Reisinger, "When should a Christian Leave a Church?", 1.
3   Ibid., 12.

institutions. Never is such deportment permissible in elders. Our Chief Shepherd has said, "Ye know that the princes of the Gentiles exercise authority upon them. But it shall not be so among you!" (Mat. 20:25, 26).[4]

Finally, at the conference Reisinger said:

> The last thing I want to mention deals with what you and I as individuals can do to help promote the truth that has become so precious to us. I believe it is time to take some positive steps to deliberately make known new covenant theology more effectively and on a wider scale. This is what we did twenty-five years ago with the truth of sovereign grace, but unfortunately, we then allowed ourselves to be side tracked from preaching the doctrines of grace to building organizations that we proudly labeled "True New Testament churches." We became institution oriented instead of grace oriented....
>
> There is a sense in which "law/grace/Sabbath" is not really the heart of the present controversy among Reformed Baptists. It is, in some cases, a smoke screen that men use to keep their congregation from discussing the whole issue of authority and liberty of conscience. This is not always the case. Some Godly men are concerned with what they feel (wrongly but sincerely) is real doctrinal error. However, some men see their personal power destroyed if their view of eldership is wrong. These men drag the Sabbath out as a red herring.
>
> What can be done by an individual if it is absolutely impossible for him to even get a hearing for the truth in his local assembly? We must do in the present situation with the truth of new covenant theology exactly what we did when we came to believe the doctrines of grace, and men and churches refused to have anything to do with us. We can all do three things.
>
> 1. We can use our voice to testify and witness to the truth of God's grace that has set our conscience free...

---

4   Ibid., 12.

2. Above all, we must demonstrate this truth and power in holy living and then testify that our life is motivated by love to our blessed Lord and Saviour. In the days of the Anabaptist, men were suspected and labeled as heretics only because they refused to submit to the state church as the "duly authorized authority" of God. Since they were so truly Godly in their life, their enemies could find nothing wrong with them.....

The legalist is not concerned with the reality of holiness itself as much as he is with the means by which it is attained. He is not willing to trust the power of the gospel in the hands of the Holy Spirit to produce a zeal for holy living; he must seek to put your neck under the yoke of law....

3. The third thing we can do is help produce and distribute the truth in printed form, tape cassettes, and video cassettes. One of the greatest tragedies of our past efforts as Baptists was our use of nothing but Presbyterian literature....We taught people the doctrines of grace, and then we gave them nothing but books written by Covenant Theologians.[5]

In 1987, Reisinger moved the John Bunyan Conference to Lewisburg, Pennsylvania. They met at the retreat center at Bucknell University, and ladies from the Reformed Baptist Church brought in food. Since that time, this conference has been held annually, almost without interruption. In 1993, the conference was held at Cowan, Pennsylvania. From 1994 to 2006, Fred Zaspel hosted the conference in New Ringgold, Pennsylvania. While at New Ringgold, they met at the Blue Mountain Christian Retreat. In a tribute to Reisinger, Zaspel relates how they met:

Around 1990 John received a paper that I had written on the subject of the law of God. Up to that point we were not acquainted with each other or for that matter scarcely knew the other existed. But after reading the paper he called and invited me to speak at the John Bunyan Conference, and there a friendship began that has continued since. In the years since I have appreciated John's love for younger

---

5   Ibid., 16–20.

ministers, his passion for truth, and his giftedness in preaching with real profit to new converts and older preachers alike. Similarly in his writings he has very effectively taught and ministered both to young believers and mature theologians (italics Zaspel's).[6]

By the end of their stay at New Ringgold, over 300 people were attending the conference. However, when they moved back to Lewisburg, John Reisinger limited the scope of the conference to NCT. This decision cut the number of regular attendees in half. Due to declining health, the last conference that Reisinger attended was in 2012. Nevertheless the pastor at Reformed Baptist Church in Lewisburg, Pennsylvania, Les Clemens, continued to hold the annual John Bunyan Conference there until 2014.

NEW COVENANT MEDIA

In the late 1980s, Gary Long and John Reisinger taught regularly at Grace Community Church in Silver Spring, Maryland. Through their ministry Jacob Moseley learned about NCT and became convinced of the necessity to promote new covenant theology literature. Therefore in 1988, Moseley became the general manager for the Sound of Grace ministries. Then in 1997, he was instrumental in establishing New Covenant Media, a publishing house for new covenant theology books, which remained in operation until 2014.

JOHN G. REISINGER

In 1988, Reisinger started *Sound of Grace*, a magazine that was published ten times a year until November, 2014. Its purpose

---

6   Fred G. Zaspel, "Why Do We Sin? Thoughts from James on Sovereignty, Sin, and Grace," in *Ministry of Grace: Essays in Honor of John G. Reisinger*, edited by Steve West, 171 (Frederick, MD: New Covenant Media, 2007).

was to promote NCT. Reisinger's book, *The Sovereignty of God in Providence*, is available in three languages. Eventually the audio-video *Doctrines of Grace Teaching Series* and the *God of the Bible Series* would receive worldwide distribution.[7]

Crowne Publications of Southbridge, Massachusetts, published *Tablets of Stone* in 1989. The New Covenant Media version was published in 2004. This is the first NCT book deliberately written to teach its position on law and grace. Reisinger warns that our understanding of Scripture should be the biblical text itself, not what the creeds state. Therefore he quotes Scripture to show how the Ten Commandments constituted the covenant document that established Israel as a nation. He concludes by saying:

> The greatest single tragedy that arises from misunderstanding the place and function of the Tables of the Covenant in the history of redemption is the assignment of a function to those tables that God never gave them. The Bible clearly teaches that the law must be cast out of the conscience before there can be true holiness in a believer's life. Bunyan, following Paul in Galatians 4, insists we must "cast out the law." One of the pressing questions in discussion of law and grace is this: How could the 'holy, just and good' law of God ever produce the mob of legalist work-mongers who crucified our blessed Lord? One of the answers is simple. Why must Hagar be cast out of Abraham's house? Why cannot the son of Hagar, a bondwoman and a type of the law (Gal. 4:21–31), be included in the inheritance with Isaac? Hagar was a wonderful handmaid, but she was never meant to be the mother of Abraham's children. The law of God is a wonderful and essential handmaid of the gospel, but was never meant by God to be the mother of holiness....
>
> Every attempt to produce holy living by applying Moses to the conscience is an attempt to give Moses a job God never

---

7   John G. Reisinger, "John G. Reisinger on the 200th Issue of Sound of Grace," *Sound of Grace*, 2.

intended him to have. It also denies the true bridegroom his full rights as the new husband.

The issue at hand is not if holiness is essential. All parties in the debate agree that of course it is! The disagreement lies in the content of the only message that can be imposed on the heart and conscience to produce fruit that will be acceptable to God. One group says: No Moses, no holiness. I say: All Christ, holiness guaranteed. The function of the law was to convict of sin and produce death....When we misunderstand the function of the law, we not only miss its true work, but we miss the greater glory of the New Covenant; that Jesus Christ is the fullest and final revelation of God's character.[8]

New Covenant Media published *Abraham's Four Seeds* in 1998. This book is the most popular best-selling book on NCT, and God has blessed it by sending it around the world. In the introduction Reisinger explains:

As New Covenant Theologians, we believe that historic Dispensationalism, as a system, is not biblical (even though it contains truth and is held by many godly men) simply because its basic presuppositions are either assumed or wrongly deduced from their theological system. We are also convinced that Covenant Theology, as a system, is just as unscriptural for the same reasons (even though it also has truth and many godly exponents). Until recently most people felt that one had to believe one or the other of these two systems.

Many people today, especially young pastors from various backgrounds, are exegeting the Word of God and discovering that one does not have to be locked into either Dispensationalism or Covenant Theology. They are also discovering that the Reformation, great as it was, never totally got rid of all of Rome's errors. Some great men brought some 'priestcraft' over into their basic presuppositions at the time of the Reformation. Their view of the relationship between church and State (the

---

8   John G. Reisinger, *Tablets of Stone & The History of Redemption* (Frederick, MD: New Covenant Media, 2004), 134, 135.

doctrine of Sacralism) is the logical conclusion and application of their Covenant Theology. It is this view that kept the Puritans from establishing churches that could live and worship consistently in the spirit of the New Covenant.[9]

GEOFF VOLKER

Geoff Volker grew up in a Roman Catholic family and attended Catholic school. In 1970, shortly before his junior year at Penn State, Volker accompanied a friend to a Gospel meeting. He could feel God convicting him; he immediately felt like a changed person and came to faith in Christ. He soon became involved with Campus Crusade for Christ, an organization serious about discipleship.

When Volker came home to Pittsburgh during the summer vacation, he met a Presbyterian youth pastor who had attended Covenant Theological Seminary in St. Louis, Missouri. At the time this seminary had just over one hundred students. The youth pastor's description of the seminary impressed him so that he decided to go there after he had graduated from Penn State. While at the seminary, he learned about and embraced the doctrines of grace and covenant theology. After graduation in 1975, he became a Presbyterian minister in Cincinnati, Ohio.

Later, through Bible study, Volker rejected infant baptism and accepted only believer's baptism. Therefore at the beginning of 1976, Volker left the Presbyterian Church. This was a difficult decision for him because he did not know where he belonged. For a while, he and his wife lived with her father, who was the pastor of the Wheaton College Church. In 1977, a church in North Fairfield, Ohio, called him to be their pastor. While he

---

9   John G. Reisinger, *Abraham's Four Seeds* (Frederick, MD: New Covenant Media, 1998), ii.

was visiting another church in 1978, he came across the *Baptist Reformation Review*. This magazine opened his eyes to another error of covenant theology—the idea that the Sabbath commandment applies to Christians today. Then, in the early 1980s, he read the theological papers presented at the Dallas Councils on Biblical Theology in *The Sword and Trowel*.

Volker first met Jon Zens who helped him appreciate the big picture and how to "do church." Afterward he met John Reisinger who enabled him to understand exactly what NCT was all about. Although these pastors helped him crystallize his thoughts, Volker did not publicly call himself a new covenant theologian until around 1990.

In 1984, Volker, along with others, started a ministry on the campus of Arizona State University. They called their ministry, "The Whitefield Society," after George Whitefield (1714–1770), an influential evangelist who believed in the doctrines of grace. Whitefield was responsible for preaching in the revival known as the Great Awakening of 1740 in the American colonies. In 1990, this ministry moved off campus and became "In-Depth Studies." This title fit their purpose, to dig deeper into the Scriptures, not just scratch the surface. Today Volker's ministry has influence around the world. Since 1996, he has regularly traveled to Eastern Europe for conferences. He has a blog, and he provides audio and video material available for free on his website. One year he hosted a weekend radio show to present NCT. For many years Murray McLellan headed up In-Depth Studies in Saskatchewan, Canada. Recently Volker started a new In-Depth Studies center in the Carolinas with Brad Woodlief. Volker holds one conference and two theological seminars every year.

To date, most new covenant literature has been concerned about the law/grace controversy. Volker is forging a new path with replacement theology that teaches how the church has replaced the old nation of Israel. Thus his studies consider continuity and discontinuity with respect to dispensationalism. To that end he is currently working on a book entitled, *Picture-Fulfillment: A Study in New Covenant Theology.*

In July 2014, Volker and the other elders at the New Covenant Bible Fellowship in Tempe, Arizona, updated their work entitled, *The New Covenant Confession of Faith*, first published online in 2007. As far as I know, their confession is the most detailed of any modern new covenant confession of faith. However, Volker is not the only modern pastor in the NCT movement to systematise his beliefs in a statement of faith. Gary George of Southbridge, Massachusetts, did this for his church. Volker writes:

> Let's now turn to the key Scriptures that the Lord used to change the direction of my theological thinking. On the issue of the Sabbath it was *Hebrews 4*. On the subject of the Ten Commandments it was *2 Corinthians 3*. On the comparison and contrasting of the Old and New Covenants it was *Galatians 3–4* and *Hebrews 7–10*. On the issue of Israel it was *Romans 9–11*. On the subject of the law it was *Ephesians 2:11–18* and *1 Corinthians 9:20–21*. The drawing power of NCT in my life was that every point of the system was clearly based in Scripture in context. At the end of the day my primary concern is to be biblical. I came out of the system of Covenant Theology where the key building blocks of the system were not based on clear Scripture but rather inferential arguments. I am thankful to say that New Covenant Theology is not established in that manner.[10]

---

10 Geoff Volker, e-mail message to A. Blake White, May 22, 2012.

CARL B. HOCH, JR.

In 1995, Carl B. Hoch, Jr. was a professor of New Testament at Grand Rapids Baptist Seminary. In the preface of his book, *All Things New*, he writes:

> This book represents the fruit of my thinking over the last twenty years of teaching. It reflects on a part of biblical theology that I have come to recognize as a very significant theme in the New Testament, newness....
>
> I was not prepared, however, for the discovery I made when I began to look for scholarly works on the subject of newness and other topics covered in this book. I found that only one substantial work had been devoted to newness, the volume by Roy Harrisville published by Augsburg Publishing House in 1960. It was distressing to find commentaries and other theological literature not developing the *theological* significance of such basic concepts as *new teaching, new covenant, new commandment, new creation, new man, new Jerusalem, new heaven and new earth, and "all things new."*...
>
> The purpose of this book is to show that newness is a topic of biblical theology that needs exploration and exposition.... The church of Jesus Christ can only move forward theologically when her members interact with one another. The death knell of theological development is the attitude that "old is good enough." If the church is to experience the dynamic newness her Lord inaugurated, she cannot stifle the Spirit who guides her into all theological truth by tenaciously embracing theological systems as absolute.[11]

So far, all the literature on NCT had originated from those within the Reformed Baptist background. Hoch was the earliest to write about the newness of the new covenant from within a dispensational setting. His book was a welcome step toward a

---

11 Carl B. Hoch, Jr., *All Things New: The Significance of Newness for Biblical Theology* (Grand Rapids, MI: Baker Books, 1995), 7, 8.

NCT understanding of Scripture. Nevertheless because of his dispensational presuppositions, he struggled with the future of Israel and admitted he had a problem that he was unable to resolve. Hoch writes:

> Just exactly how "all Israel" will be saved is not spelled out by Paul or any other New Testament writer. It has been the contention throughout this discussion that salvation is only in Christ. So this eschatological group must believe the gospel of Jesus Christ. They will also enjoy all the blessings that Christ has secured through his death, burial, and resurrection. And they will receive those promises God made to Israel in the Old Testament that they have not yet enjoyed such as possession of the land of Palestine. Their position in terms of Jews and Gentiles within the church at present is not clear. The pre- or posttribulational rapture of the prior group creates problems with terminology for "all Israel." Should they be called church? Saints? People of God? Or some other title? What should believers prior to the Exodus be called? This is a problem for any system, not only premillennialism. But an acute problem for premillennialism because the millennial kingdom will include believers who were not raptured and resurrected when the church was raptured and resurrected…What label can a premillennialist give this group of redeemed? This writer does not believe that biblical revelation to this point offers enough clear information to come to a conclusive decision on the problem.[12]

THE SEARCHING TOGETHER CONFERENCE

In 1995, Jon Zens held the first Searching Together Conference in Dresser, Wisconsin, with the theme, "The Church in the World." Zens applied NCT perspectives to the history of how the Puritans in the new land of America treated the natives. He explains:

---

12 Ibid., 317, 318.

Old Covenant typology dominated: the Puritans exiting England paralleled Israel leaving a land of bondage, crossing the Atlantic paralleled the Red Sea exodus, arriving on the shores paralleled Israel's entering a land flowing with milk and honey, and the Natives that met the Puritans paralleled the heathen nations Israel faced. A major dilemma developed for the Puritan leaders. The Old Covenant typology pointed in the direction of casting the Natives out of the land, while the New Covenant pointed toward evangelizing these people. Should they kill those who stand in the way of their inheriting the land, or preach the Gospel to them? Tragically, in the overall picture, the Old Covenant won the battle, and many Natives were liquidated as time elapsed in the name of claiming the New Land for the newcomers.[13]

Then in 1999, Zens held the second Searching Together Conference in Chatsworth, California, with the theme, "Foundations of New Covenant Theology." Four of the speakers were Darryl Erkel, Daniel Thompson, Geoff Volker and Jon Zens. Since 2011, Zens has hosted the conferences in Elgin, Illinois. The sixteenth conference occurred in June 2015.

GARY D. LONG

In 2001, Gary Long self-published *Context! Evangelical Views on the Millennium Examined.* He carefully explains and examines various views on eschatology. Then he describes what he means by New Covenant non-premillennialism.[14] To date, no one else had explained the principles whereby a new covenant theolo-

---

13 Jon Zens, e-mail message, March 28, 2015.

14 Historic premillennialism, dispensationalism, and progressive dispensationalism are various forms of premillennialism. Most covenant theologians believe in either postmillennialism or amillennialism; some are premillennialists. Postmillennialists believe Christ will return after the millennium. Amillennialists believe the millennium referred to in Revelation 20 means the era between the two comings of Christ. I prefer the term, non-millennial over new covenant non-premillennialism.

gian figures out the truths found in the Bible. In *Context!* Long defines how a new covenant theologian interprets Scripture:

> The interpretation of Scripture by New Covenant non-premillennialists agrees with the grammatical-historical approach emphasizing context. It also agrees with three principles: the primacy of the New Testament over the Old, of clear texts over those which are highly symbolical and not so clear (especially apocalyptic texts), and the *now-not yet* principle. It also recognizes and emphasizes the importance of discerning the importance of biblical parallelism in literary structure to help determine the theological point of a given passage.[15]

TOM WELLS AND FRED ZASPEL

By the year 2000, more people knew about and believed in NCT—to the distress of covenant theologians. That is why Richard Barcellos wrote his book, *In Defense of the Decalogue: A Critique of New Covenant Theology* in 2001. Meanwhile Tom Wells and Fred Zaspel had met at the John Bunyan Conference in March 1993 when John Reisinger had invited them both to speak. They became good friends. Shortly after Barcellos' book was published, they decided to collaborate on a comprehensive book explaining NCT. Wells and Zaspel did not want to merely review Barcellos' book but present substantial reasons for the existence of NCT. They list five points in the preface of *New Covenant Theology*:

> First, it has seemed to some of us that if the New Testament is the apex of God's revelation, then we ought to read the earlier parts of Scripture in its light....Second, the NT is very explicit in making believers "slaves" of Jesus Christ....Third, a nagging question arises when OT law becomes too prominent in discussions of Christian moral and ethics....A fourth thing calls for an understanding of NCT: the renewed emphasis in our day on

---

15 Gary D. Long, *Context!*, 295.

exegetical and biblical theology as the source of systematics....
Finally, in one of the odd providences that the Lord sometimes
sends our way, those who defend New Covenant Theology find
themselves falling in with an emphasis that has been prominent
throughout church history.[16]

Although they did not feel the necessity of responding
to Barcellos directly, they do mention three difficulties that
Barcellos has with NCT:

> *First*, New Covenant Theology is not a monolithic movement....
> *Second*, New Covenant Theology is a relatively new school of
> thought and has yet to *hit the press*.... *Third*, one major adherent
> of new Covenant Theology has recently acknowledged that he
> will have to modify his understanding of the Old Covenant and
> revise some of his published works (italics Barcellos').[17]

Fred Zaspel wrote six chapters in *New Covenant Theology* on
the law of God. In one chapter he explains:

> Some have concluded that all of Moses' law, except the ceremo-
> nial aspects, remains binding on the New Covenant believer.
> Some have concluded that "the moral law" of Moses remains
> intact while the civil and ceremonial laws have passed away.
> Some have assumed that *all* of Moses remains binding *unless
> specifically repealed* by Jesus or the NT writers. Still others have
> assumed that *nothing* of Moses remains binding *unless specifi-
> cally restated* by Jesus or the NT writers. In one sense the confu-
> sion is entirely understandable, for the NT writers both "abol-
> ish" Moses' law and continue to enforce many of its commands.
> It would seem that the NT writers want to have Moses and not
> have Moses all at the same time!
>
> But the Gordian knot is easily undone when it is understood that
> Jesus is to Moses what the butterfly is to the caterpillar. Moses is
> not struck down. Moses did not "fall" (Luke 16:17). Nor was he

---

16 Tom Wells and Fred Zaspel, *New Covenant Theology*, 1, 2.

17 Richard Barcellos, *In Defense of the Decalogue: A Critique of New Covenant
    Theology* (Enumclaw, WA: Winepress, 2001), preface; cited by Tom Wells
    and Fred Zaspel, *New Covenant Theology*, 3.

"destroyed" (Matt. 5:17). Moses is "fulfilled." In Christ, Moses reaches maturity and emerges in full bloom. Moses' law still has relevance, but only as it comes to us from the hands of the Lord Jesus. Christians today must still read Moses, and for great profit, but when they read him they must be careful to wear their Christian lenses. Moses' law is not simply incorporated into the New Covenant as it was revealed through Moses—it is fulfilled, advanced, and brought to completion.

Plainly stated, Christ does not relegate Moses to the status of a museum showpiece. Neither should we expect to find Moses with the same status today that he enjoyed before the coming of Christ. Having been fulfilled, he is surpassed, and it is our pleasure today to read his law in the shape given it by the Lord Jesus Christ....

Finding how a given law from Moses receives treatment by Jesus and/or the NT writers demands attention to detail. But this is the interpreter's task exactly—he must use his entire Bible. The law of Moses finds its fulfillment in the law of Christ, and we must look to see *how* this is so in any given case (italics Zaspels').[18]

In the Foreword Douglas J. Moo, a professor and New Testament scholar, writes, "Wells does a fine job of analyzing some of the historical and broadly theological issues..."[19] For example, Wells writes:

A *mathematical* unity suggests that each of the covenants functions in the same way, much as links in a chain do....

A *teleological* unity, however, would work in a different way. It would be a unity in which each covenant contributed something to the fulfillment of redemptive history, but what each contributed could be quite different from the contributions of the other covenants. For example, the Noahic (sic) Covenant

---

18 Fred Zaspel, "The Continuing Relevance of Divine Law," in *New Covenant Theology*, 157–160.

19 Douglas J. Moo, " Foreword," in *New Covenant Theology*, xiii.

(Gen. 9:8–17) provided a continuing earthly scene on which redemption could take place. The Abrahamic Covenant with its promises outlined the course of redemptive history, while setting forth two kinds of redemption and two peoples to experience them. Then the Mosaic Covenant regulated the course of redemptive history by producing the people who would write the Scriptures and bring forth the Messiah. Each of these covenants, if they did no more than I have suggested here, would serve the same ultimate purpose, to bring glory to God in the salvation of a people that no man can number....

The goal of God's redemptive activity is the New Covenant. Each preceding covenant had its part to play in redemption's story....

Finally, "in the fullness of time," God sent forth his Messiah, the agent of his eternal salvation toward which all of history tended. *Already* this Messiah, the Lord Jesus, is creating a new nation to inhabit a new heavens and a new earth. The citizens of that nation are the members of God's universal church, now united to the Lord Jesus in the body of Christ. Beyond this lies glory. It is not yet clear to us what all that will mean. "But we know that when he appears, we shall be like him, for we shall see him as he is" (1 John 3:2) (italics Wells').[20]

In 2005, Wells wrote *The Priority of Jesus Christ* to emphasize the logical priority of the New Testament over the Old. He asks, "In what sense is Jesus Christ first in your life as a believer in him? Closely related to that is a second question: In what sense is Jesus Christ to come first in our understanding of Scripture?"[21]

AN OPEN LETTER TO DR. R. C. SPROUL

In September 2002, R. C. Sproul's magazine, *Tabletalk*, carried five articles against antinomianism. Richard Barcellos

---

20 Tom Wells, "Appendix Two: The Relations Between the Biblical Covenants," in *New Covenant Theology*, 276–280.

21 Tom Wells, *The Priority of Jesus Christ* (Frederick, MD: New Covenant Media, 2005), 2.

wrote "The Death of the Decalogue" in which he called Tom Wells, Fred Zaspel and John Reisinger Antinomian. Because Sproul had indirectly maligned them publicly, John Reisinger felt compelled to respond to Barcellos' article in *Tabletalk* on the Sound of Grace website. Therefore he wrote an open letter to Dr. R. C. Sproul:

> We welcome all open discussion on the subject of law and grace. We are especially grateful to you for clearly defining, in the article by Morton Smith (pages 8–10, 54), what was historically considered antinomianism. We can only wish you had used that definition consistently throughout the entire issue instead of having it discarded for new and different definitions, especially the definition used by Richard Barcellos....
>
> I agree with you that true antinomianism is a heresy and a failure by church leaders to label it as such is a sin against Christ and his Church....However, to either falsely accuse someone of this heresy, or to use an inaccurate definition when labeling someone an antinomian is also a sin against Christ and a fellow believer. Morton Smith, on page 10 of *Tabletalk*, quotes a work entitled *Antinomiamism Discovered and Confuted* by Thomas Gataker, a member of the Westminster Assembly, that lists six marks of antinomianism. Not a single one of the six things on that list are true of Tom Wells, Fred Zaspel or me. One of the six could conceivably apply, but only if our view was misunderstood. The other five are far off our convictions. Your magazine's articles, especially the one by Barcellos, that use our name in print, rest their case on two major points. First, we disagree with Covenant Theology's view of the Sabbath (as does John MacArthur, and did Calvin, Luther, James M. Boice, and others), and second, we believe Christ is a new lawgiver who, in revealing more fully and completely the character of God, not only raises the Law of Moses to a higher and more spiritual level, but also gives the church some new laws.
>
> I do not at all enjoy writing in a public forum against a fellow believer whom I deeply respect. However, since you chose to

use that setting to criticize me as a proponent of New Covenant Theology, I felt appropriate to respond in kind.

Let me clearly spell out my view of the Ten Commandments. I ask you to show me what I believe that deserves your condemnation of me as an "antinomian" heretic.[22]

Then Reisinger goes through the Ten Commandments, one by one, and discusses what the New Testament Scriptures teach about them. He concludes by saying:

Tabletalk's readers could infer from the September issue that its authors and editor would fall into the camp that labels any view but that of classical Covenant Theology as antinomianism. We would echo Dr. Boice's plea for tolerance and acceptance, and above all urge all involved to openly discuss the biblical data instead of sticking an undeserved label on those who disagree with a creed.[23]

As far as I know, Sproul never responded to that letter. He certainly never changed his views on strict adherence to the Westminster Confession.

PROVIDENCE THEOLOGICAL SEMINARY

In 2003, Pastor Joe Kelley of Killeen Bible Church in Killeen, Texas, and Pastor Jackson Boyett of Dayspring Fellowship in Austin, Texas, wanted to help unify and enhance the development of NCT as a theological system; they decided to establish a graduate-level seminary with those goals in mind. Therefore they approached Gary Long and asked him to consider establishing such a school. Kelley explains:

---

22 John G. Reisinger, "An Open Letter to Dr. R. C. Sproul," 1, 2, last modified (date), accessed August 28, 2013, http://solochristo.com/theology/nct/reisinger-lettertosproul.htm.

23 Ibid., 11.

As pastors, both Jackson and myself, struggled with where to send young men who felt the call of God to enter the ministry. We both loved Westminster in Philadelphia, but were concerned about the stress on traditional Covenant Theology which students receive at that otherwise great institution. The Dispensational seminaries, such as Dallas, Grace, Trinity, Masters and others were considered deficient because often times these schools are not fully Calvinist, plus we disagreed with the Dispensational understanding of how the Bible structures itself. We never really gave much thought to the Baptist Seminaries; I guess because we just assumed they would overly stress loyalty to the denominational line in their teaching and fail to help students become independent thinkers. However, for my part, I am thrilled with what is coming out of Southern Baptist Seminary in Louisville, Kentucky, and would have no problem at all in recommending that school to anyone seeking training for the ministry.[24]

By 2007, Gary Long had taken steps to organize and form such a seminary in Colorado Springs, Colorado. With the name of Providence Theological Seminary, it completed its 4th year of academic studies in May 2011.[25] In 2012, Providence Theological Seminary celebrated the graduation of its first M.Div. student, Zachary Maxcey.

This seminary exists to promote NCT, the doctrines of grace, and Baptist theology. During the planning stages in 2004–5, Gary Long entered into an agreement with Michael Haykin, principal of Toronto Baptist Seminary. This was an important liaison for both seminaries. Because Toronto Baptist Seminary has existed since 1927, Dr. Haykin was glad to extend its influence into the United States and assist a new Calvinistic Baptist Seminary. Moreover Dr. Long states:

---

24 Joe Kelley, e-mail message, August 18, 2014.
25 Gary D. Long, "New Covenant Theology: What it is and How it Differs from Covenant Theology," 16.

In short, the relationship with Dr. Haykin and TBS came about because of mutual respect for one another in standing for sound doctrine as expressed by those of us who are forging ahead with New Covenant Theology as a more accurate way to understand the way of God (Acts 18: 26), especially regarding covenantal administration of the law of God and the progressive outworking of God's eternal purpose via biblical covenants.[26]

Providence Theological Seminary began sponsoring bi-annual Councils on Biblical Theology in Colorado Springs beginning in 2009. The purpose of these conferences was to further establish NCT as a more accurate way of understanding the Scriptures.[27] Then in July 2014, this conference moved to Grace Church, Franklin, Tennessee. The theme was "God's Eternal Purpose: NCT—Time for a More Accurate Way." At the end of it, the pastor, William W. Sasser, Jr., announced that his church intended to host this conference annually, which they did in July 2015.

In 2010, Gary George, the pastor of Sovereign Grace Chapel in Southbridge, Massachusetts, became the eastern representative of the seminary. In November 2014, the seminary published its first issue of the *Providence Theological Seminary Journal* with Zachary Maxcey as the editor. He also serves as the Social Media Administrator and oversees the seminary's blog. In addition, by 2014, the seminary began offering online courses. Then in May 2015, Gary Long moved Providence Theological Seminary to Franklin, Tennessee, to be co-located with Grace Church at Franklin.

---

26 Gary Long, e-mail message, May 30, 2014.
27 Gary Long, e-mail message, September 12, 2014.

A. BLAKE WHITE

Blake White grew up in a non-Christian home with no preconceived ideas of the Bible. In 2001, he was converted to Christ his freshman year of college in Temple, Texas.

In 2004, he took a semester off of college to evangelize in universities. Since he did not know anyone in most of the cities in which he stayed, he would often read all evening that whole semester. Having recently learned of God's exhaustive sovereignty, he began questioning many of his previous presuppositions, including baptism. He benefited greatly from many Presbyterian theologians and was reconsidering his current Baptistic views.

During that semester of evangelism, he would visit likeminded churches. He ended up at Mills Road Baptist Church in Houston, Texas. On the recommendation of the pastor, he bought *Abraham's Four Seeds* from a book stall that sold books in the church library. After he had finished reading it, he asked Pastor Larry Newcomer for more books. The pastor gave White *New Covenant Theology* by Wells and Zaspel. By the end of 2004, White called himself a new covenant theologian. That same year White felt God calling him to the ministry of the Word. Therefore he searched for a Baptist seminary espousing the doctrines of grace and found the Southern Baptist Theological Seminary in Louisville, Kentucky.

White began his studies in the fall of 2006. That first semester, Steve Wellum taught White the NCT storyline in his hermeneutics class. In addition, White took classes with Thomas Schreiner, also a new covenant theologian. In 2007, White took biblical theology from Dr. Wellum. During the summer, he worked on a paper entitled, "The Newness of the New Covenant," for the class.

When he had finished the paper, he wanted to share it with others. Therefore he sent the manuscript to John Reisinger. He was pleasantly surprised when Reisinger phoned him and asked him to present the paper the following spring at the 2008 John Bunyan Conference. White has been a regular speaker at the conference ever since. He has also contributed regularly to the *Sound of Grace*. New Covenant Media published *The Newness of the New Covenant* in 2008. In 2010, White wrote his second book, *The Law of Christ: A Theological Proposal.* By 2014, New Covenant Media had published ten of his books. Moreover, Reisinger also promoted White on the Sound of Grace website.

CHAPTER 7
LATER LITERATURE AND EVENTS

In 2007, Dennis M. Swanson, director of the Master's Seminary Library, wrote a paper to introduce the major players in the NCT movement. Up until that time, all the books and literature were either self-published or published through New Covenant Media, a publishing company under the auspices of Sound of Grace. Swanson felt this movement could not have much influence until a major evangelical publishing company would begin to publish NCT authors. By 2009, professors like Jason C. Meyer and James M. Hamilton, did begin publishing books with a NCT leaning in major publishing companies. However, none of those professors actually used the words NCT.

In 2011, this movement suffered a setback when Moe Bergeron and others separated over a disagreement on the way the Holy Spirit works in the life of a believer. Up until now, John Reisinger has spent most of his time distinguishing NCT from covenant theology. By 2011, he began to discuss the differences between NCT and dispensationalism.

JOHN G. REISINGER

In the *Sound of Grace* John Reisinger wrote a series of articles on continuity and discontinuity between the Old and New

Testaments in 2010. He did this to compare NCT and covenant theology. At the following John Bunyan Conference he preached on this subject and also published it as a book, *Continuity and Discontinuity*. The advertisement in the *Sound of Grace* states:

> The subject of Continuity and Discontinuity is one of the "hot button" issues in reformed theology today. How many of the laws in the Old Testament are Christians to obey today, and how many of those laws are fulfilled and done away in Christ?...
>
> Our Lord changed some laws, dropped some laws, and added some laws. He never once contradicted Moses. He did contrast his new higher law with Moses. However, contrasting and showing something is better is not contradicting. The real issue involved as the author demonstrates in this book is this: Does Jesus replace Moses as a new lawgiver in the same sense that he replaces Aaron as high priest? Is Jesus a new lawgiver, or is he merely the final interpreter of Moses? Does Moses rule the Christian's conscience as the final authority on morality, or is that throne occupied by Christ alone?
>
> If we discuss covenants, there is 100% discontinuity. The Old Covenant, in totality, has been replaced by the New Covenant. If we discuss God's one unchanging purpose in sovereign grace, there is 100% continuity.[1]

In the November 2011 issue of *Sound of Grace*, Reisinger began a series of six articles on NCT and prophecy. Then in the July—August issue in 2012, he wrote a series of articles on Christ, our new covenant Prophet, Priest and King. New Covenant Media published *New Covenant Theology & Prophecy* in 2012. This book also discusses the issues of continuity and discontinuity between the Old and New Testaments. But this time Reisinger compared NCT with dispensationalism. The advertisement in the *Sound of Grace* states:

---

1   John G. Reisinger, *Continuity and Discontinuity*, advertisement in *Sound of Grace*, no. 176, (April 2011): 11.

If we primarily use the Old Testament Scriptures to form our understanding of eschatology, we likely embrace a premillennial understanding of Abraham's and David's expectations. At the risk of over-simplifying, we will refer to this as a Dispensational hermeneutic. If we use texts in the New Testament Scriptures that deal with the promise to Abraham we likely will favor the amillennial position. Again, at the risk of over-simplifying, we will call this a Covenant hermeneutic (short for Covenant theology). Currently, New Covenant theology has no clearly defined hermeneutic. Adherents of New Covenant theology have attempted to answer this question by modifying either Covenantal hermeneutics or Dispensational hermeneutics.

One of the basic presuppositions of New Covenant theology is that the New Testament Scriptures must interpret the Old Testament....This book represents an attempt to begin serious work toward establishing New Covenant hermeneutics from the ground up—that is, without beginning with either Covenantal or Dispensational hermeneutics.[2]

By April 2014, John Reisinger had published twenty-four books through New Covenant Media—the latest one being *The New Covenant Church—Ekklesia—of Christ*.

FRED G. ZASPEL

In 2011, Zaspel wrote *The New Covenant and New Covenant Theology*. The summary on this book's back cover states:

In this book, Fred Zaspel explores the provisions of the New Covenant and expounds its implications for life and worship as well as for biblical interpretation. By doing so, he provides a clear guide for understanding the "big picture" of the Bible and an exulting appreciation of the glorious privileges that belong to every Christian. He also shows that the inauguration of the

---

2   John G. Reisinger, *New Covenant Theology & Prophecy, Sound of Grace*, no. 196, (April 2013): back cover.

New Covenant is the hinge of biblical and redemptive history and that its promises define the nature of the privileges of the people of God and their status in Christ.[3]

MOE BERGERON

The law/grace controversy in Dallas was influential in his understanding of NCT. However, he disliked all of the infighting, and he still feels as if there are a lot of unresolved issues.

At the end of the John Bunyan Conference in April 2011, Fred Zaspel took part in a panel. Anyone at the meeting could ask anything they wanted. Someone asked him what the greatest danger was for NCT in the future. He replied that new covenant theologians were a tiny part of Christendom, and we need to stick together. We should not become divided.

I wondered what issue threatened to split up this small group of believers. After the meeting was over, I asked Moe Bergeron if Fred was talking about eschatology. I knew people did disagree about the end times. He answered, "No, the Holy Spirit, but it is nothing to worry about." Although I was puzzled by his answer, I did not ask him what he meant. The next thing that I knew, Bergeron ended his online relationship with Reisinger at the end of 2011. He had been supporting the Sound of Grace website for many years.

In 2015, I conducted a phone interview with Bergeron in preparation for this book. He explained to me why he stopped paying for the Sound of Grace website: In 1992, Bergeron heard John Piper speak at a conference. Afterward Bergeron asked Piper if he could post his sermons online. Piper gladly gave him ten years of his sermons. As a result Piper was one of the first

---

3   Fred G. Zaspel, *The New Covenant and New Covenant Theology* (Frederick, MD: New Covenant Media, 2011), back cover.

to have his sermon outlines on the Internet in 1995. Bergeron saw the Internet as a way of making the Word of God free for people all over the world. Over time he built up a sermon library of Piper's sermons. So many people accessed those sermons that Piper became well-known around the world.

Then, in 1996, Bergeron began chat rooms to discuss NCT. He also created a new website with the same domain for both Sound of Grace and John Piper. Traffic to Piper's sermons benefited Sound of Grace. When Jacob Moseley started New Covenant Media in 1997, Moe Bergeron thought that John Reisinger was making a huge mistake by not giving away the digital copies of his books as did John Piper. In 2001, Bergeron advised Piper to establish his own sermon library. Meanwhile Bergeron continued to send traffic to the Sound of Grace website through his own website, Christ My Covenant.

PICTURE-FULFILLMENT NEW COVENANT THEOLOGY

In the fall of 2011, Maxcey wrote a paper entitled, "Picture-Fulfillment New Covenant Theology: A Positive Theological Development?" for a special studies course taught by Dr. J. David Gilliland and Dr. Gary D. Long at Providence Theological Seminary. In so doing, he brought to the forefront a dispute simmering quietly among new covenant theologians. In June 2009, Chad Bresson had posted on Moe Bergeron's blog:

> Fulfilling Isaiah 42 and 49, this King becomes The Covenant himself, his own promise and guarantee to His people, bestowing all the rights and privileges of kingdom citizenship. Entry into this kingdom, must be through the One who is Covenant

Himself, the only One with the authority to bestow the rights and privileges of kingdom citizenry.[4]

Then in November 2010, Bresson posted sixty-three tenets of NCT. Maxcey quotes two of them in his paper:

> 22. The New Covenant is not like the covenant made with the people through Moses. Embodied and personified in Christ, the New Covenant brought into existence through the life and cross work of Christ is made with his redeemed people through grace. God's people do not enter the New Covenant by works, but by grace through faith; it is radically internal, not external; everlasting, not temporary.

> 43. Christ is the Law of the New Covenant, incarnating the new standard of judgment as to what "has had its day" in the law and what has abiding validity (Col. 2:17). The Holy Spirit is the indwelling Law of Christ, causing New Covenant members to obey Christ the Law in conformity to His image.[5]

However, Bresson expanded on his tenets in May, 2011, as follows: Tenet 22 became tenet 31. Tenet 43 became tenet 55.[6] Therefore, although Maxcey cited the older version of Bresson's NCT tenets, he did quote him correctly. Maxcey explains:

> Advocates of Picture-Fulfillment NCT are emphatic in stressing that it is essential for the New Covenant believer to understand the 'Christ is the Covenant' principle if they are to experience a

---

4   Chad Bresson, "The Exceeding Righteousness of the New Covenant," 8, last modified (date), accessed January 19, 2015, http://christourcovenant. blogspot.ca/2009/06/exceeding-righteousness-of-new-covenant.html.

5   Chad Bresson, "What Is New Covenant Theology?", 2, 4, last modified (date) accessed January 19, 2015, http://breusswane.blogspot.ca/2010/11/ what-is-new-covenant-theology.html; cited by Zachary S. Maxcey, "Picture-Fulfillment New Covenant Theology: A Positive Theological Development?", 3, last modified (date), accessed November 2, 2015, http://www.ptsco.org/Picture-Fulfillment%20NCT.pdf.

6   Chad Bresson, "What Is New Covenant Theology?", 3, 4, last modi-fied (date), accessed January 19, 2015, http://breusswane.blogspot. ca/2011/05/what-is-new-covenant-theology.html.

dynamic Spirit-filled life. Regarding the 'necessity' of this doctrine, Bresson states:

> Because *Christ has become a Covenant for His people* and the *Spirit* has descended to indwell Christ's people as *the law written on the heart*, there is an altogether new dynamic inherent to the question of New Covenant ethics. No longer do imperatives find their impetus from without as was true of the Mosaic Code (exemplified in the Tablets of Stone), but from within. *The nature of the command itself is no longer external, but internal.* Obedience isn't acquiescence to an external demand, but the manifestation of an inward reality (italic's Bresson's).[7]

Bresson presented his paper, "The Incarnation of the Abstract: New Covenant Theology and the Enfleshment of the Law," at the July 2011, New Covenant Theology Think Tank in Rushville, New York.[8]

The Earth Stove Society published online, *The 4ᵗʰ Stream: Introducing the 4ᵗʰ Stream within New Covenant Theology: A Minority Opinion* by Chad Richard Bresson, Edwin W. Trefzger III and a special word from Murray McLellan, on January 3, 2012. They dedicated the book to John Reisinger. Meanwhile Reisinger published Maxcey's paper in two parts in the *Sound of*

---

7   Chad Bresson, "The Incarnation of the Abstract: New Covenant Theology and the Enfleshment of the Law," 2, 3, last modified (date) accessed January 19, 2015, http://www.ncbf.us/thinktank2011/TheIncarnationoftheAbstract-NCTThinkTank2011.pdf; cited by Zachary S. Maxcey, "Picture-Fulfillment New Covenant Theology: A Positive Theological Development?", 3.

8   Joseph Krygier explains on his church's website (New Covenant Baptist Fellowship, Evans NY), that this conference originally began as small meetings in 2003 and 2006, sponsored by In-Depth Studies. However, Krygier continued to sponsor these meetings from 2007 onward as think tanks to develop new covenant thinking. In 2013, he moved the conference to a larger venue to accommodate more people. Then in 2014, he renamed the conference, All Things New.

Grace Issues of February and March 2012. Then in the March issue of *Sound of Grace*, Reisinger wrote:

> I hesitate to criticize the advocates of this new view. They are godly sincere brothers. These people have embraced and unashamedly taught NCT. They have stood shoulder to shoulder with us in promoting the glory of NCT. Ostensibly their goal is to magnify the person and work of Christ. Many of the leaders of the Fourth Stream are personal friends for whom I have the deepest love and respect. They recently posted a book on the Fourth Stream and dedicated it to me.[9]

In a footnote he commented that it was awkward having a book dedicated to him when he did not agree with its message! He made it plain in his article that *Sound of Grace* does not endorse this new view. He stated:

> My first problem with the Fourth Stream is the fact that it seems to violate an essential principle of NCT, namely, that we must interpret the OT with the NT. The foundation texts used to establish this new idea by the Fourth Stream is found in two texts in Isaiah....Isa. 42:6...Isa. 49:8.

> It is quite clear that these two Scripture texts in the Book of Isaiah use the phrase "give thee for a covenant;" however, no NT text either directly quotes or refers back to these two verses as a fulfillment....

> The question is whether the two Isaiah passages are to be understood ontologically or metaphorically. The word *ontological* means a word or phrase is to be understood in a literal sense. The word *metaphorical* means the opposite. It means a word or phrase should be taken as a figure of speech. Christ "lay down his life for the sheep" is metaphorical; it does not mean Christ died for four legged animals....Isaiah 42:6 says two things were given, a "covenant" and a "light." The text says *I will give thee for a covenant of the people, a light for the Gentiles.* No one would

---

9   John G. Reisinger, "A Critique of the New View of NCT," *Sound of Grace*, no. 185 (March 2012): 2.

suggest that the word *light* in this text was to be understood in a literal sense....

The Fourth Stream is built on the insistence that the words *give thee for a covenant* must be taken in an ontological sense. They say it must mean that Christ is literally the actual covenant.....

My second problem with the Fourth Stream is its view of the work of the Holy Spirit in sanctification....

Before I accept the Fourth Stream's new idea that the Holy Spirit is "one and the same" as the "law written on the heart" I need a text or two unpacked that proves that statement is true. I think we have every right to expect something in John 14–16, where Jesus laid out some clear teaching on the ministry of the Holy Spirit, to show the evidence of the new view's claims that the "Spirit has descended to indwell Christ's people as the 'law written on the heart.'" There is not a shred of textual evidence in the New Testament for the Fourth Stream's claim of its novel view of the Holy Spirit being "one and the same" as the "law written on the heart."...

The Holy Spirit is the teacher. He is not the lesson. The Holy Spirit does not decide on what to teach, He teaches the curriculum given to him by the Son. "He [the Holy Spirit] will not speak on his own; he will speak only what he hears" (John 16:13). There is no way these verses can be made to mean that the Holy Spirit is "one and the same" equal to the law written on the heart....

We agree that the *entire motivation* to obey God's new covenant commands is internal via the Holy Spirit, but the commands are not discerned by an immediate work of the Holy Spirit but by external inspired commands....Every command comes to us in words. God's commands to us as new covenant believers do not constitute some fuzzy, emotional, mystical experience that is centered inside of us, but all commands are verbal and objective. They all come to us externally and not internally....

It would be very wrong to accuse the Fourth Stream of deliberately downgrading the authority of Scripture but it surely seems to be one of the implications of their view. Granted, they constantly affirm there are imperatives in the new covenant but in the same breath they insist there are no external commands in the new covenant. They can't have it both ways.

At the end of the day, we might ask one question. How do you understand this text?

Circumcision is nothing, and uncircumcision is nothing, but the keeping of the commandments of God 1 Cor. 7:19 (italics Reisinger's).[10]

Furthermore in *Kingdom through Covenant*, Peter Gentry explains how Isaiah 55:4–5 teaches that the future David will be a witness to the nations. His comments shed greater light on the meaning of the word "covenant" in Isaiah 42:6 and Isaiah 49:8. He writes:

> A lexical study of *ʿēd* shows that a witness functions in *covenant* relationships, especially with a view to restoring broken relationships....This is what the Davidic King is for the nations. Note that in the Servant Songs, twice the Davidic King is informed that he will become in his person a covenant with the people (Isa. 42:6; 49:8). Just as the term "witness" can sometimes replace "covenant," so the "ark of the covenant" becomes the "ark of witness," so here: to say that David is a witness to the peoples is correlative to the statements in the Servants Songs that he is a covenant to the people (italics Gentry's).[11]

GARY GEORGE

In 2012, New Covenant Media published Gary George's book, *Hermeneutical Flaws of Dispensationalism*. Until recently, the focus has been primarily on exposing the errors of covenant theology. George writes in his preface:

---

10 Ibid., 4, 6, 16, 23.

11 Peter J. Gentry, in *Kingdom through Covenant: A Biblical-Theological Understanding of the Covenants*, 414, 415.

I had been an avid supporter of J. N. Darby's (1800–1882) Classic Dispensationalism for eleven of my sixteen years among the Plymouth Brethren; I abandoned it almost twenty-five years ago. As a dissident of Classic Dispensationalism, I am not surprised to hear that prominent men have renounced that weak theological system. My own switch originated in August 1986, not by means of men's writings, but through a commentary-less study in the Book of Romans....

Turning back to the first chapter of Romans, I realized that the first two verses confirmed my could-be-new-heresy. "...the gospel of God (which he had promised afore [O.T.] by his prophets in the Holy Scriptures)..." (Rom. 1:1–2). I was almost afraid to read further for fear that what I might find would destroy my career and relationships among the Brethren and other fellow Dispensationalists. Nevertheless, I continued to read, seeking to believe all things written in the Book, even if the consequences of what I believed distanced me from the most esteemed of saints. For me, the Roman epistle settled the verdict; I saw not only there, but also everywhere throughout the New Testament Scriptures, that the church and church age is indeed the subject of prophecy in the Old Testament Scriptures.[12]

GARY D. LONG

In 2013, Long published *New Covenant Theology: Time for a More Accurate Way.* He defines NCT in this way:

"New Covenant Theology" (NCT) is a developing system of theology that is working to provide a more accurate way of interpreting the Scriptures than that taught by the systems (including their internal variations) of traditional Covenant Theology (CT) and Dispensational Theology (DT). NCT is a biblical theological approach to understanding the progressive unfolding of the history of redemption in fulfillment of God's eternal kingdom purpose on earth. This approach is based upon

---

12 Gary George, *Hermeneutical Flaws of Dispensationalism* (Frederick, MD: New Covenant Media, 2012), 11, 12.

a Christ-centered *Christotelic*[13]... interpretation of the Bible, both Old and New Testaments, that emphasizes the way in which the New Testament interprets the Old as taught by the risen Christ to the Emmaus disciples when "He explained to them the things concerning Himself in all the Scriptures" (Luke 24:27). While agreeing with aspects of CT and DT, NCT questions the basic hermeneutical presuppositions of both theological systems, neither of which are consistent in interpreting the OT in light of Christ in the NT. The fundamental difference that New Covenant Theology has with the traditional system of Covenant Theology is over its one *overarching* Covenant of Grace designed to support the churches existence in the OT and infant baptism of covenant children in the NT, and over its teaching of the threefold division of God's law into *moral, ceremonial and civil (judicial)*. The fundamental difference with the system of Dispensational Theology is over its teaching of two redemptive purposes—one for Israel and one for the Church—and explanation of unfulfilled Bible prophecy. The differences that NCT has with both systems also relate to the doctrine of the Church and the meaning and significance of Spirit baptism (italics Long's).[14]

So far, Dr. Long has published six books because of his concern for the doctrines of grace and NCT.

THE MODERN GRACE MOVEMENT

At the 2011 Providence Theological Seminary Conference, Dr. J. David Gilliland presented a paper entitled, *New Covenant Theology: Is There Still a Role for the Imperatives?* The *Sound of Grace* published it in issues 183 and 184, December/January 2011 and February 2012. Because of the feedback that he received from his paper, he decided to critique the "Modern

---

13 The word "Christotelic" results from the combination of two Greek words: Christos meaning Christ and telos meaning end or goal.

14 Gary D. Long, *New Covenant Theology: Time for a More Accurate Way* (Charleston, SC: www.CreateSpace.com, 2013), 179, 180.

Grace" movement in the *Sound Of Grace* in 2013 in a series of three articles. In the first article he explains:

> *Law* in the New Testament Scriptures—when juxtaposed with grace or gospel—is never mere command but always the "Mosaic Code" as a whole, with the pejorative phrase *works of the Law* being typified by unbelieving Israel and ultimately reflective of the unregenerate man or woman's attempt at being right with God by self-effort, independent of a personal faith and trust in God Almighty....

> The phrase *obedience to Christ* means many things. We obey Christ when we follow his example. We obey Christ when, in good conscience, we follow the leading of the Spirit and apply the general principles of the Word of God. And we obey Christ in the more restricted sense when we obey specific commandments in the written word, all various aspects of the law of Christ or God's law for his New Covenant people. And in using God's law in this manner, we are not equating it with the Mosaic code....

> This discussion, from my perspective, is about the legitimacy and need for intentionally or volitionally obeying any written commandment or principle, even those in the NT....

> That is one of the key aspects of the "Grace Movement," namely, that joyful communion with Christ and any understanding of law or commandment that included the believer's volitional response to the Word of God are mutually exclusive....

> On the one side of the spectrum, we have the Federal Vision, which confuses justification with sanctification and understands justification to be a process, undermining the principles of imputation and *Sola Fide*. At the other end of the spectrum, we have the "Grace Movement," those that want to make sanctification an accomplished process, one separate from and often contrasted with intentional obedience to the written word. Now there is no denying that in one sense we constantly look back at our justification as the foundation of our new life, but that is different than reducing sanctification to justification. And in

fact, it is not uncommon for many to simply deny that sanctification can even be described as a process at all....

But what happens if we equate "the Word" and intentional obedience with "the way of the written code"? That is in essence what is happening in the broader "Grace Movement." And with respect to the role of the Scriptures in the life of the church, what would you expect to be the result? At the end of the day, the central issue has to do with the role of Scripture, including the imperatives or commands, and the human will as God-ordained means the Spirit uses in the sanctification process. And although certainly unintended by most, *Sola Christo* is being pitted against *Sola Fide* and *Sola Scriptura* (italics Gilliland's).[15]

You may be wondering what the "Grace Movement" has to do with a NCT history. Gilliland outlines five specific characteristics of the "Grace Movement":

1. New Obedience

2. Historical-Redemptive Reductionism

3. Love vs. Commandment Reductionism

4. The Conflation of Justification and Sanctification

5. A reductionism that separates a relationship with Christ from the legitimate use of God-ordained means—the written word, church offices/officers/ordinances, and even the regenerate human will.

Concerning historical-redemptive reductionism, Gilliland writes:

What is the result if we posit a different kind of obedience, an obedience that transcends or excludes an intentional or

---

15 J. David Gilliland, "The New Heart, The New Covenant, and Not So New Controversies: A Critique of the Modern 'Grace Movement,'" Part 1 of 3, *Sound of Grace*, no. 197, (May 2013): 7, 13, 18.

volitional response to the written word? It results in a "Historical-Redemptive" reductionism. Within the "Grace Movement" in general, including some who use the term NCT, there is an increasing tendency toward a Barthian type theology, one that promotes unbiblical implications and applications regarding the legitimate distinction between the Word of God and the Incarnate Word, as well as the increasing exclusivity of the redemptive story or "Historical-Redemptive" paradigm....

In one blog interaction I was asked, "Is the living Christ of greater value to his saints than the written Word?" First of all, the question illustrates another characteristic of this movement: the fallacy of the "either-or." My answer was and is, "In the believer they are never separated."...The authors of Scripture never separated them when referring to the walk of the believer with God. The written Word of God is the vital tool of the Spirit, one that in his hand is part of the indispensable *whole armor of God* (Eph. 6)....

And for some in the broader "Grace Movement" as it is generally used, it has come to a point of not only reducing the Christian life to "who Jesus is" or "what He has done"—to the exclusion of what he has commanded or instructed—but to simply the "cross event" (italics Gilliland's).[16]

He concludes:

And most importantly, they have opened the door to a theology that undermines the role of the Word of God and the principle of *Sola Scriptura*, one that rejects or minimizes the reality of the regenerate human will and ultimately the principal of *Sola Fide* and the doctrine of justification by faith alone (italics Gilliland's).[17]

---

16 J. David Gilliland, "The New Heart, The New Covenant, and Not So New Controversies: A Critique of the Modern 'Grace Movement,'" Part 2 of 3, *Sound of Grace*, no. 198 (June 2013): 12, 18.

17 J. David Gilliland, "The New Heart, The New Covenant, and Not So New Controversies: A Critique of the Modern 'Grace Movement,'" Part 3 of 3, *Sound of Grace*, no. 199 (July-August 2013): 19.

After reading Gilliland's assessment of the "Grace Movement," I am concerned about how their teachings will lead believers down a slippery path of error. They have created two classes of believers: those who pay attention to the written Word for their guidance and those who believe that the Holy Spirit will lead them into all truth without relying on Scripture. When one says that the Holy Spirit will reveal all truth to a person only internally, believers may find the Holy Spirit has revealed something to them that differs from what he has revealed to another.[18]

ACADEMIC WRITINGS

According to Dennis M. Swanson in 2007, the lack of mainstream publications of NCT has limited its widespread influence in evangelicalism. Up until that point, all books on NCT were published by New Covenant Media or self-published.[19] Recently, however, the academic world has begun to publish relevant books although the professors prefer to discuss biblical theology rather than NCT. Stephen Wellum and Peter Gentry use the term "progressive covenantalism" in reference to NCT. Nevertheless all these professors employ the redemptive- historical storyline espoused by NCT.

---

18 Helpful books on the role and function of the Holy Spirit are: James M. Hamilton Jr., *God's Indwelling Presence: The Holy Spirit in the Old and New Testaments* (Nashville, TN: B & H, 2006); Gary D. Long, *Context! Evangelical Views On The Millennium Examined*, 3rd ed (Charleston, SC: www.CreateSpace.com, 2011); Michael A. G. Haykin, *The Empire of the Holy Spirit* (Memphis, TN: Borderstone Press, 2010).

19 Two exceptions are: an article by Douglas J. Moo, "The Law of Christ or The Law of Moses," in *Five Views on Law and Gospel* (Grand Rapids, MI: Zondervan, 1996); and D. A. Carson, ed., *From Sabbath to Lord's Day: A Biblical Historical and Theological Investigation* (Eugene, OR: Wipf & Stock, 1999), but originally published by Zondervan in 1982.

B & H Academic published Jason C. Meyer's book, *The End of the Law: Mosaic Covenant in Pauline Theology*, in 2009. The summary on the book's back cover states:

> Commonly understood as the first theologian of the Christian faith, Paul set forth the categories by which we describe our relationship with Christ. Did he understand the new covenant Jesus announced at the Last Supper primarily as a replacement of the old Mosaic covenant God made with Israel, or as a renewal and completion of the old? Jason Meyer surveys the various differences that have been argued between the two covenants in *The End of the Law,* carefully and inductively performing a semantic, grammatical, and contextual analysis of all the Pauline texts dealing with covenant concepts.[20]

Crossway published James M. Hamilton Jr's book, *God's Glory in Salvation through Judgment: A Biblical Theology*, in 2010. The summary on the book's back cover states:

> In Exodus 34 Moses asks to see God's glory, and God reveals himself as a God who is merciful and just. James Hamilton Jr. contends that from this passage comes a biblical theology that unites the meta-narrative of Scripture under one central theme: God's glory in salvation through judgment.
>
> Hamilton begins in the Old Testament by showing that Israel was saved through God's judgment on the Egyptians and the Canaanites. God was glorified through both his judgment and mercy, accorded in salvation to Israel. The New Testament unfolds the ultimate display of God's glory in justice and mercy, as it was God's righteous judgment shown on the cross that brought us salvation. God's glory in salvation through judgment will be shown at the end of time, when Christ returns to judge his enemies and save all who have called on his name.
>
> Hamilton moves through the Bible book by book, showing that there is one theological center to the whole Bible. The volume's

---

20 Jason C. Meyer, *The End of the Law: Mosaic Covenant in Pauline Theology* (Nashville, TN: B&H Academic, 2009).

systematic method and scope make it a unique resource for pastors, professors, and students.[21]

Crossway published Peter J. Gentry and Stephen J. Wellum's book, *Kingdom through Covenant: A Biblical-Theological Understanding of the Covenants*, in 2012. The summary on the book's back cover states:

> The disciplines of biblical and systematic theology join forces to investigate anew the biblical covenants and the implications of such a study for conclusions in systematic theology.

> By incorporating the latest available research from the ancient Near East and examining implications of their work for Christology, ecclesiology, eschatology, and hermeneutics— Biblical scholar Peter Gentry and systematic theologian Stephen Wellum present a thoughtful and viable alternative to both covenant theology and dispensationalism.[22]

Baker Academic published Thomas R. Schreiner's book, *The King in His Beauty: A Biblical Theology of the Old and New Testaments*, in 2013. The summary on the book's back cover states:

> Thomas Schreiner, a respected scholar and a trusted voice for many students and pastors, offers a substantial and accessibly written overview of the whole Bible. He traces the storyline of the Scriptures from the standpoint of biblical theology, examining the overarching message that is conveyed throughout. Schreiner emphasizes three interrelated and unified themes that stand out in the biblical narrative: God as Lord, human beings as those who are made in God's image, and the land or place in

---

21 James M. Hamilton Jr., *God's Glory in Salvation through Judgment: A Biblical Theology* (Wheaton, IL: Crossway, 2010).

22 Peter J. Gentry and Stephen J. Wellum, *Kingdom through Covenant: A Biblical-Theological Understanding of the Covenants* (Wheaton, IL: Crossway, 2012).

which God's rule is exercised. The goal of God's kingdom is to see the king in his beauty and to be enraptured in his glory.[23]

---

23 Thomas R. Schreiner, *The King in His Beauty: A Biblical Theology of the Old and New Testaments* (Ada, MI: Baker Academic, 2013).

CHAPTER 8

SPREADING INTO CANADA AND AROUND THE WORLD

In my first book, *A Tale of Two Kingdoms*, I traced Jesus as the promised Seed throughout Scripture and paid close attention to the timeline. I did not realize I had written a biblical theology book until Dr. G. A. Adams, late principal of Toronto Baptist Seminary, told me. Sometime later, a pastor friend told me that I should go to the John Bunyan Conference. I had never heard of it. At the conference in 2008, I realized my book followed the historical-redemptive timeline of NCT. I rejoiced in finding like-minded people and looked forward to attending the conference every year.

In 2013, someone asked me why so many Canadians attended the conference. I replied that John Reisinger was Canadian. A short time later, I discovered he was American. However, because he had spent time as a pastor in Canada, he influenced many Canadians.

JOHN REISINGER IN CANADA

When a young woman from Toronto, Ontario, decided to attend Bible College in Wheaton, Illinois, she had no idea how God would use her to influence others. At Wheaton she met a young man from Lewisburg, Pennsylvania, who attended the Reformed

Baptist Church where John Reisinger was pastor. After they became serious, the young man invited her to Lewisburg. While there, she heard the doctrines of grace for the first time. She was upset at the idea of God's sovereignty in salvation and threatened to break up with the young man. But she changed her mind.

The young woman attended Long Branch Baptist Church (a church in The Fellowship of Evangelical Baptists of Canada). In 1959, this congregation was searching for a new pastor. Because of the recommendation of this young woman, Reisinger became their pastor for seven years, from 1959 to 1966.

In 1959, few, if any pastors among the Fellowship Baptists in Ontario, believed in the doctrines of grace. By the time Reisinger left Long Branch, that church family wholeheartedly embraced those truths. When they interviewed their next pastor, Ray Reed, they made sure that he believed them as well. Sadly, after he left, subsequent pastors did not preach those truths.

While Reisinger was in Toronto, he took a few courses at Toronto Baptist Seminary. In addition, he often spoke for the Christian Business Men's Association. As a result of those speaking engagements, the Fellowship Baptist Church in Woodstock called him to be their pastor. They did not realize his position on the doctrines of grace, however. He remained there for two years and afterward returned to an itinerant ministry in the United States.

During Reisinger's last one and one half years at Long Branch, Jim Clemens became the assistant pastor. Thus began a close relationship lasting to this day. In 1972, Jim Clemens purchased fifty acres north of Marmora, Ontario, where he intended to build his future retirement home. Meanwhile he developed Rockwood Bible Camp. Every summer for twenty-five years Reisinger preached at that camp. In the evening they would sit around the campfire and discuss theology. Over time they changed from talking about the doctrines of grace to NCT.

Jim Clemens appreciated the gracious way in which John Reisinger convinced others of the truths in Scripture. He recalls how Reisinger played golf every Monday with men from the Long Branch congregation and discussed Sunday's sermon.

Jim Clemens influenced his brother Les, who was also a pastor, to accept NCT. Two of Jim Clemens sons, Les and Jim, became pastors and also preached those truths. Jim's brother, Les, remembers how Reisinger quietly talked to someone at Rockwood who questioned him about the doctrines of grace. His gentleness in dealing with others impressed Les.

THE WELLUMS

Both Colin and Joan Wellum came from Presbyterian families. After God saved them in an evangelical church, they attended an Associated Gospel Church in Burlington, Ontario. As a chiropractor Colin became friends with many people. Don Wheaton was one friend who gave Colin the *Sovereignty of God* by Arthur W. Pink. Someone else gave them other books. Through those books they learned about the doctrines of grace and wanted their four boys taught God's truth.

In 1970, William Payne, the pastor at Calvary Baptist Church in Burlington, hosted a conference. Joan decided to go to that conference although she did not attend that church. Colin wanted to go but said that he had to see his patients in the evenings. However, when he twisted his ankle, he had to cancel his office visits for a couple of nights and, as a result, was free to attend the conference with Joan. The Wellums appreciated John Reisinger's message at the conference and sent him a donation for *The Sword and Trowel*. Reisinger phoned to thank them for giving him confirmation that he should continue publishing the paper.

Although it was difficult to leave their friends, they soon left the Associated Gospel Church and began attending Calvary Baptist. When Calvary split over the doctrines of grace, the Wellums left with William Payne to help found Trinity Baptist Church.

The Wellums owned a triplex and told Reisinger that he could stay on their upper floor whenever he wanted to, which he did. This was a tremendous blessing for Joan and Colin and their four sons. He often stayed there on his way to a conference in Canada. Once he stayed for two weeks while Colin treated Reisinger's frozen shoulder.

Reisinger had a great influence on the whole family. Two of their boys, Colin and Jonathan, are in secular work but serving the Lord. Kirk is the eldest. He became a Christian in 1975. His parents were extremely influential in teaching him about the Bible. He never had a problem believing the doctrines of grace, and he appreciated the ministry of many gifted pastors. He began teaching at Toronto Baptist Seminary in 2006. Then in 2008, he became their interim principal after Michael Haykin left Toronto for the Southern Baptist Theological Seminary. In 2009, Kirk was officially appointed principal.

Concerning John Reisinger, Kirk Wellum writes:

John Reisinger was very influential at key points in my life where he sat and listened to me, answered my questions and then explained some things to me about the way the Bible was put together that I did not understand that well. What John said helped fill in the pieces of the biblical puzzle and helped me integrate what I had discovered as a result of my own study and through reading scholars like D. A. Carson. During this time my brother Stephen and I had lots of long conversations about these things as well. I already had a good grasp of "New Covenant Theology" before Roger [Fellows] assumed the leadership of the SGF.[1]

When Stephen went to school at Roberts Wesleyan College for three years, he attended Reisinger's church in Rochester. Later, when Stephen married, Pastor John officiated the ceremony. Stephen is a professor at the Southern Baptist Theological Seminary in Louisville, Kentucky. As you can see, John Reisinger has had a direct influence in spreading NCT—first, from the United States into Ontario, and then back into the States.

WILLIAM PAYNE

In 1959, Dr. Harold C. Slade, the pastor of Jarvis Street Baptist Church and president of Toronto Baptist Seminary, spoke at a church in Liverpool, England. At the end of the service, Dr. Slade said he thought someone in the congregation was interested in training for Christian service. William Payne was interested in Christian training, but not in Canada. He went home and told his wife what had happened. They both rejected the idea of moving to Canada and tried to forget it. But six weeks later he and his wife Hetty found themselves on their way to Toronto. Once there, they had two problems: amillennialism and the doctrines of grace were foreign ideas to them. Since they were teachable, however, they stayed and learned with an open mind. Before long, they came to believe both those truths.

In July of 1964, Payne became the pastor of Calvary Baptist Church (a Fellowship Baptist Church) in Burlington. At that time he began to read the Puritans and discovered more about

---

1   Kirk Wellum, e-mail message, July 15, 2014. SGF stands for Sovereign Grace Fellowship.

Calvinism. As time went on, he faced increasing opposition over his Calvinistic teaching so that he had to resign in the fall of 1972. Some of the congregation followed him and founded Trinity Baptist Church.

A few other pastors in the Fellowship also left because of opposition to their belief in the doctrines of grace. Some managed to stay, however. Therefore in the summer of 1972, William Payne, Leigh Powell, Gord Rumford and Roger Fellows formed a reformed pastors' group F.R.P.S. (Fellowship for Reformation and Pastoral Studies). In 1978, Payne became the chairman and from then on the unquestioned leader. By 1983, Payne felt that the Reformed Baptist churches needed a more formal fellowship. Therefore the Sovereign Grace Fellowship of Baptist Churches came into being with six founding churches. These churches could have ties with other denominations as long as they did not belong to the World Council of Churches. From the beginning Payne encouraged fellowship with independent churches and with others involved in different denominations.[2]

ROGER FELLOWS

Roger Fellows came from England in 1963 while working in the Pharmaceutical industry. Then in 1966, he studied part time at Toronto Baptist Seminary for one year. When controversy broke out between Jon Zens, Walter Chantry and Al Martin in the late 1970s, Fellows began to study the issues for himself. The negative feelings between these pastors disturbed him.

Fellows attended the Harvey Cedars Conference in June 1979 where Walt Chantry preached on "The Kingdom of God." This is his assessment of Chantry's messages:

2   Roger Fellows, "Bill Payne and the Sovereign Grace Movement in Canada," 1–4, 6, 7, 14, unpublished paper, n.d.

I was actually at the conference where Walt Chantry gave the messages later developed into his book, *God's Righteous Kingdom*. He was attempting to deal with two extremes: on the one hand, the Zens approach to Covenant Theology, and on the other, Reconstructionism or Theonomy as advocated by Greg Bahnsen in his main book, *Theonomy in Christian Ethics*. I think Chantry attempted too much and didn't do a very good job of either. Of course, most agreed in opposing Reconstructionism; so the focus became the so-called antinomianism of Zens. Perhaps Zens went too far but his ideas certainly spawned the renewal of New Covenant Theology. Not only did the controversy sharply divide the Reformed community, especially in the U.S., but it created hard feelings, generally on the part of those holding to Covenant Theology, towards those holding a New Covenant view. Sadly that controversy was soon followed by the authoritarian controversy that separated, for example, Al Martin and Walter Chantry.[3]

In 1994, Fellows returned to England for five years. While there, one of the deacons at his church circulated *Tablets of Stone* by John Reisinger within the congregation. This stirred up controversy in the church, but dealing with this issue crystallized Fellow's thoughts on NCT and on the Sabbath issue.

After William Payne had unexpectedly passed away in June of 1997, there was a vacuum in the leadership of the Sovereign Grace Fellowship. Meanwhile in 1999, Roger Fellows had come back to Canada. By 2001, the Sovereign Grace Fellowship became a legal entity in the eyes of the government. At this point Fellows assumed the role of co-ordinator.

In Ontario, any controversy always came down to whether or not the Sabbath was an abiding moral law. Many a discussion quietly took place around the camp fire after Reisinger spoke at Rockwood Acres. To address this issue Fellows wrote a pamphlet

---

3   Roger Fellows, e-mail message, January 23, 2015.

entitled, "The Law and The Christian," in 2002. These are his subject headings:

1. All people are at all times subject to God's laws.

2. Sin is defined in terms of law.

3. We must not equate God's unchanging laws with the law of Moses.

4. The whole Mosaic law is abrogated or cancelled under the new covenant.

5. As already stated, this does not leave the believer without law.

6. God's moral requirements for people do not change substantially.

7. The place of the Sabbath.

Concerning the Sabbath, Fellows writes:

> We are often told that the Sabbath is "God's abiding, unchanging moral law." My response to that is to ask who really believes that? The Mosaic command, as we saw, was to keep the seventh day holy. Who does that apart from Seventh Day Adventists and a few others? Those who broke the command were to be stoned to death. Who applies that today? Whatever people say, those who believe the Sabbath applies to Christians, change it from the form in which it was given, so how can it be abiding and unchanging?[4]

Fellows concludes with these thoughts:

> Having set out briefly what I believe about the place of the law in a believer's life, I would also like to make the point that it

---

4   Roger Fellows, "The Law and The Christian," 6, unpublished pamphlet, March 26, 2002.

should not be a point of great contention and certainly not a test of fellowship. This is a complex issue and one that has divided Christians for centuries....

We may be fully convinced of our own view, but we must also allow others to be fully convinced of a different view. As Christians, we can often agree to differ over baptism; we can agree to differ on views of the Lord's return: surely we can agree to differ over the Lord's Day/Sabbath issue. With a perishing world around us that needs the gospel, we must not spend time fighting over secondary matters. Love must prevail.[5]

By 2014, fifteen churches have joined the Sovereign Grace Fellowship—fourteen in Ontario and one in New Brunswick. I have been told that most pastors in the Sovereign Grace Fellowship agree with the teaching of NCT. However, they do not use that expression—preferring to agree to disagree with Reformed Baptists who hold to the Ten Commandments as God's unchanging moral law.

RENÉ FREY

René Frey is the son of William-Henri Frey, who came from Switzerland to study at Toronto Baptist Seminary. After his studies he returned to Switzerland, but twelve years later the French wing of the Fellowship of Evangelical Baptists (AEBEQ)[6] asked him to return to work for the Lord in Quebec. His journal Le Phare (The Lighthouse) was an important evangelical tool for many years. As a result his son René Frey grew up in Quebec.

René was one of the first 110 students who completed SEMBEQ's[7] first course, An Inductive Study of the Gospel of Mark

---

5   Ibid., 11, 12.

6   Association d'Églises Baptistes Évangéliques au Québec

7   The Fellowship Baptist French Language Seminary: Séminaire Baptiste Évangélique du Québec

in 1974. He loved studying God's Word and felt the call of the Lord on his life. Since SEMBEQ could not yet offer the courses that he needed, he went to France to become a full-time student at Faculté Libre de Théologie Évangélique (The Free School of Evangelical Theology). When he returned to Quebec, Frey began to teach some courses to students in Chertsey. For thirty-five years he was the pastor of a local church in Montreal and a teacher at the seminary. This followed the paradigm of training that SEMBEQ had adopted—to keep future leaders within their local churches during the duration of their training. The Lord has blessed this model for training pastors.

Frey taught Greek, Eschatology, and Bibliology (the study of the Bible) for SEMBEQ. In November 2014, SEMBEQ published a book to celebrate its forty year anniversary. This book states that Frey "helped to revise the guided study courses and he defended the doctrines of grace as well as New Covenant Theology."[8]

Frey knew Les Clemens and Jim Clemens and his sons through the Fellowship of Evangelical Baptists. Moreover John Reisinger and Geoff Volker influenced Frey in his understanding of NCT. In addition, he attended the John Bunyan Conference in Pennsylvania.

SEMBEQ has always had a bias toward premillennialism. Frey himself taught non-millennialism. Jean-Guy Poisson, Michelle Poule, and Mrs. Hurtubise (Marion Ford) collaborated on a course on amillennialism. The seminary offered a course comparing the three views: amillennialism, progressive

---

8 René Frey, ed., *SEMBEQ: 40 Years: Celebrating the Faithfulness of God*, (Montreal, QC: SEMBEQ, n.d.), 39.

dispensationalism, and non-millennialism.[9] The seminary also presented sixty-six lessons in disk format by John MacArthur in which he flipped out all the OT prophecies to the end times. Frey made a sixty-seventh disk to teach non-millennialism.

Presently the six pastors at Église Baptiste Évangélique de Rosemont in Montreal are actively promoting NCT. Moreover in January 2015, Frey wrote:

> I have just asked our Seminary (Sembeq) to invite Professor Doug Moo a day earlier than planned for his course on Romans in order to give a workshop on New Covenant Theology. I was impressed a few years ago in reading the chapter by Doug on a modified Lutheran view of the relationship of law to gospel in *Five Views on Law and Gospel*. The assistant director François Turcotte told me it would not be possible for this round of teaching on Romans 1–8 in March. But next time, when Doug comes to finish the teaching on this epistle, Sembeq will ask him for that. I would try to line up some of our Fellowship pastors (Steve West, Clemens and others) for the same date to have a more complete description of that approach for our QC pastors.[10]

AUSTRALIA

In 1979, Jon Zens happened to find out about some unadvertised meetings for the Seventh Day Adventists in Nashville, Tennessee; Robert D. Brinsmead was the speaker. Since 1975, Zens had been reading the paper, *Present Truth* (later *Verdict*), published

---

9   Many new covenant theologians call themselves amillennialists. But Gary Long explains why it is important to distinguish one's self from the covenant theology idea of amillennialism. He disagrees with covenant theologians for the following reasons: "(1) the role in which the "one-covenant-of-grace" theology versus "New Covenant theology" has in the redemptive outworking of the nature of the church under the New Covenant; and (2) the theological significance of baptism in/with the Spirit in forming the body of Christ." Gary Long, Context!, 294.

10 René Frey, e-mail message, January 23, 2015.

by the Seventh Day Adventists. He met with Brinsmead and Jack Zwemer in their hotel room on Friday and Sunday nights while they were at the conference. Zens writes:

> I was impressed by Brinsmead's teachable, open spirit. He obviously did not feel threatened by my pointed and probing questions. One area that I asked him about was the idea that the law had to do a "work" before the gospel could come to folks. His magazine had been permeated with this concept. I suggested that if all things are to be approached through Christ, why do we put the law ahead of Him in evangelism? Where in Acts were the Ten Commandments preached before the gospel? He said he thought I had some good points and that he would reflect upon them....
>
> In 1981 some brilliant essays appeared in *Verdict*. "Sabbatarianism Re-examined," "Jesus and the Law," and "The Heart of NT Ethics" presented a Christ-centered approach to ethics. It was certainly heartening to see this shift by the largest English-speaking theological journal in the world at that time (sadly, since mid-1984 RDB went markedly downhill).[11]

In fact, Brinsmead would become a liberal in his theology. Nevertheless he did introduce NCT ideas into Australia.

TO EVERY TRIBE

David Sitton came from a broken home whose parents divorced when he was fourteen years old. Since his parents had been raised in the Churches of Christ, they had occasionally attended as a family. At the age of eighteen he was a surfer living only for "the next wave, the next party and the next girl."[12] But Joyce Dowell was different from all the other girls. She loved Jesus. God used Joyce to open David's spiritual eyes to his need for the Savior.

---

11 Jon Zens, "Law and Ministry in the Church," *Searching Together*, 25, 26.

12 David Sitton, *Reckless Abandon* (Greenville, SC: Ambassador International, 2011), 29.

Then God used Joyce's dad to mentor him. After high school Sitton wanted to study the Bible, so he enrolled in the School of World Evangelism in College Station, Texas. While there, he met Joe Cannon, a missionary with a passion for Papua New Guinea (PNG). Joe's passion became David's passion. He writes, "From that moment, the course of my life was firmly set. I would not go where the gospel was already planted. I didn't want to build on already-laid foundations; I wanted to blaze trails in places where the gospel had not yet made its way."[13]

After two years in PNG, he came home in 1979 due to serious illness. But he wanted to go back as soon as possible—and with a wife. Sitton explains, "PNG was a tough and lonely place to live as a single young man. I often prayed for a partner in ministry."[14] Since he also wanted more education, he enrolled in the Institute of Christian Studies in Austin, Texas, and began attending Dayspring Fellowship where Jackson Boyett was the pastor. The people there prayed that God would give David a wife.

Two weeks later, Sitton spoke at a youth meeting in Harlingen, Texas. At the end of the meeting, the leader of the group asked him what he needed. Sitton replied, "A wife." The young people laughed at Sitton's honesty. But a young lady took his need to heart. Three days later he received a letter stating, "If you ever get back to this town, come see me. I've always wanted to be a missionary."[15] Soon he did meet and marry Tommi, a seventeen year old, in his uncle's church. Her father gave his blessing as long as she finished high school first. Tommi graduated in May, 1980, and they married in June.

---

13 Ibid., 37, 38.
14 Ibid., 49.
15 Ibid., 50.

Before they went to PNG, Jackson Boyett gave him books to read on election and predestination. Sitton, however, insisted that he would never believe in election. Fourteen months later, after reading those books, he did come to accept the doctrines of grace. When he and Tommi approached their sending church with this news, the church withdrew their support and informed all their other financial supporters that they were no longer missionaries.[16] This was not true. Boyett took Sitton to the Council on Biblical Theology in 1982 in Plano, Texas. For the next two years David and his wife rebuilt their support from like-minded churches.

In 1990, the Sittons were devastated to find out that PNG would not renew their missionary visa to live there full-time. David, however, was allowed to visit annually for short-term mission trips. By 1994, Boyett encouraged Sitton to train other missionaries in order to multiply his effectiveness. At first Sitton did not want to do that. However after moving to Los Fresnos, Texas, near the Mexican border, this idea intrigued him. He began leading people in short mission trips to Mexico.

In 2003, Stephen Henry and his wife Robin, from Christ's Covenant Church in Warsaw, Indiana, announced they were going to join the Sittons full-time in Los Fresnos. By 2004, To Every Tribe received official status as a non-profit organization. After the first board meeting Rod and Linda Connor, from

---

16 So many people misunderstand election. They wonder why someone who believes strongly in election would want to become a missionary. From their point of view, if God is going to save whomever he will save, no matter what, why become a missionary? I met David Sitton at the Sovereign Grace Fellowship annual meeting in 2014. He said that believing in election was a great impetus for him to become a missionary. God promised that persons from every tribe and language and people and nation would be in heaven (Revelation 5:9). Sitton is willing to risk his life to find those people who live in the remote places of the earth.

Reformed Baptist Church in Lewisburg, Pennsylvania, soon joined them full-time as well.

Since that time the mission has expanded and bought more property to train more people for the mission field. The course lasts two years with 40% of the time in class and 60% on the field in Mexico or PNG. The mission advertises itself as Baptist and Reformed. Nevertheless the staff and supporting churches believe overwhelmingly in NCT.

In 2008, To Every Tribe hosted a mission conference in Austin, Texas, with the theme: The Purpose-Driven *Death*. This has been Sitton's passion since God saved him. He concludes his book with these words:

> These are the kind of missionaries the church needs, and I'm on the lookout for them. I'm on a crusade to recruit *Navy Seals* missionaries! I want the *First Responders* for the cause of Christ, those who are willing to charge into impossible near-suicide situations, simply because Jesus and the gospel are worth the risk! (italics Sitton's).[17]

In 2014, Sitton began to make plans to send two missionary couples into northern Ontario into an aboriginal village where there is no Christian witness.

FACEBOOK

William Dicks is the moderator of the Facebook group, New Covenant Theology. He is a computer specialist living in South Africa. Dicks first came to believe the doctrines of grace and then later NCT. He did not know the label, however, and thought he was alone in his beliefs. Then in 1999 and 2000, he lived in the United States and had free Internet access. He was thrilled when he discovered solochristo.com—finally, someone else with the

---

17 David Sitton, *Reckless Abandon*, 202.

same beliefs. He only knows of two others in South Africa who believe in NCT. Therefore he appreciates connecting with others on the Internet.

In 2015, a second Facebook group called Discover New Covenant Theology began discussing issues pertaining to NCT. Some of those who joined this new group left New Covenant Grace, another group with a new covenant emphasis. However, many of the members of New Covenant Grace teach that the Holy Spirit writes the law of Christ directly on the heart without using Scripture. Thus the Holy Spirit reveals truth for believers internally, not externally through the Bible.

The Internet has become a powerful tool for people from around the world to connect with each other. New covenant theologians are taking advantage of this means of getting to know one another and of disseminating truth. Nevertheless true believers need to discern truth from error.

CHAPTER 9

PRESENT DAY EVENTS AND OBSERVATIONS

Every history must end at some point in time. I have chosen to finish this history with the retirement of John Reisinger. Nevertheless the story continues on through a younger generation. I am encouraged by Ron McKinney's report on Together for the Gospel. This generation will continue to spread the word about the proper way to put the Old and New Testaments together.

In chapter one I listed my presuppositions concerning the NCT storyline of Scripture. I believe in three important pillars of NCT: a believers-only church, the doctrines of grace, and the historical-redemptive timeline of Scripture centered in the Lord Jesus Christ. I shall conclude by stating what Zachary Maxcey means by a Christotelic interpretation of Scripture. Finally, I shall list A. Blake White and Gary Long's analysis of the important tenets of NCT—then some final thoughts on issues concerning NCT today.

TOGETHER FOR THE GOSPEL

Ron McKinney told me about the 2014 conference of Together for the Gospel; 9000 people gathered, consisting mostly of young preachers. He thinks many of them are leaning toward NCT, and

35% graduated from the Southern Baptist Theological Seminary under the influence of Albert Mohler Jr.

CROSS TO CROWN MINISTRIES

Douglas Goodin planned on a career as a songwriter/guitar player until he felt the Lord calling him into pastoral ministry. He enrolled at Covenant Seminary and completed his M.Div. at New Geneva Seminary in Colorado Springs, Colorado. He became the associate pastor of Front Range Alliance Church, Colorado Springs, in January 1999 and its senior pastor in January 2006. He founded Cross to Crown Ministries and the New Covenant School of Theology in 2010.

In March 2014, Jacob and Carol Moseley celebrated John Reisinger's ninetieth birthday with friends from the John Bunyan Conference. Blake White and Douglas Goodin have been good friends who appreciated Reisinger's ministry. One day, in conversation, they wondered who would continue what Reisinger had begun. As president of Cross to Crown Ministries, Goodin began to wonder if the Lord wanted his organization to continue Reisinger's work. During the summer John Reisinger, Jacob Moseley, Blake White and Douglas Goodin prayed, talked and considered a merger of Sound of Grace and Cross to Crown Ministries. Eventually the board overseeing Sound of Grace agreed that this merger was the Lord's will. Jacob Moseley retired from being manager of Sound of Grace while John Reisinger joined Cross to Crown Ministries. Therefore in the fall of 2014, Reisinger made this announcement:

> I wish to take this opportunity to thank you for your support of *Sovereign Grace New Covenant Ministries*, the legal corporation under which *Sound of Grace and New Covenant Media* operates. Some of you have faithfully supported our efforts for over

fifty years. We would not claim or in any way pretend that the ministry of *Sovereign Grace New Covenant Ministries* is responsible for the evident growth of both historic Calvinism and New Covenant Theology today. However, we would be exhibiting false humility if we did not acknowledge that our CDs, DVDs, books, the *Sound of Grace* theological journal and the John Bunyan Conferences have had an effect in teaching a lot of people the five doctrines of grace and the glory of the New Covenant established by our sovereign Savior. Under the blessing of God your partnership in our labors was just as essential as our teaching and writing.

With the retirement of Jacob and Carol Moseley, the time has come for *Sovereign Grace New Covenant Ministries* to find others who can manage the various administrative functions necessary to the functioning of this organization.

To that end the assets of *Sovereign Grace New Covenant Ministries* are being transferred to *Cross to Crown Ministries* of Colorado Springs, CO. This transition is currently in process and will be completed by November 2014.

I will continue to be involved in the ministry but only in an advisory capacity. We are not starting a new ministry nor are we disbanding a present ministry. We are merging two ministries that have the same goals...(emphasis Reisinger's).[1]

Then Douglas Goodin, president of Cross to Crown Ministries, paid tribute to John Reisinger and introduced his own ministry:

For many years, decades in fact, John G. Reisinger has promoted the Christ-honoring biblically faithful truth referred to as *New Covenant Theology*. His impact has been deeply significant through *Sound of grace, New Covenant Media, The John Bunyan Conference*, and other ministries. He has preached the doctrines of grace with a rare combination of pastoral compassion and

---

1   John G. Reisinger, "An Important Announcement," *Sound of Grace*, No. 211(October 2014): 14.

exegetical precision. He has endeared the hearts of numerous believers with a kind, gentle spirit befitting a shepherd of Christ's sheep. And he has taught the absolute supremacy of Jesus, even in the face of public hostility and personal opposition. Like so many others, I thank God for John G. Reisinger's tireless labor for the gospel.

But there is much more work to be done. As I preach and teach New Covenant Theology here in Colorado, I often hear two responses: *Why have I never seen this before—it's so obviously biblical?* and *Why doesn't every Christian believe this?* These kinds of questions led me to create *Cross to Crown Ministries* a few years ago, an organization committed to exalting Christ above all things. Recently, after seeking the Lord's direction for *Cross to Crown*, I set a 20-year goal to make NCT the leading hermeneutic in the world. It's ambitious, I realize, and ultimately, the results are up to King Jesus, but I believe it is a goal worthy of Him. Those of us who understand the supremacy of Christ and the greater glory of His New Covenant must continue to proclaim it. It's right. The Church needs it. The *world* needs it. Jesus deserves it.

And so I am deeply honored and excited by the opportunity to build upon the work brother John and many others have so faithfully accomplished over the years. Blake White and I have become good friends over the last few years, and I cannot wait to see what opportunities the Lord Jesus gives us to serve together for the glory of his name…(emphasis Goodin's).[2]

After the amalgamation with Sound of Grace was completed, Goodin updated the Cross to Crown website. He offers many free resources: articles, audio and video teaching. Plans are in the works for a new version of the *Sound of Grace* theological journal. Moreover the first Cross to Crown National Conference was held in June 2015.

---

2   Douglas Goodin, "An Important Announcement," *Sound of Grace*, no. 211 (October 2014): 14, 15.

WHAT IS NEW COVENANT THEOLOGY?

NCT is a biblical theology that teaches the grammatical-historical timeline of redemptive history and the centrality of Christ. Zachary Maxcey explains what a Christotelic hermeneutics means:

> A Christotelic hermeneutic views the Lord Jesus Christ as the focus and ultimate goal or end of God's Word seeking to consistently interpret all Scripture in view of this great truth (Luke 24:27). Furthermore, this particular method of interpretation emphasizes three principles: (1) the person and work of the Lord Jesus Christ is *the nexus* of God's plan in redemptive history; (2) *all* Scripture either refers to Christ *directly* (e.g., the Gospel narratives, messianic prophecies) by referring to Christ *typologically* or preparing *the way* for Christ by unfolding redemptive history which ultimately points to His person and work (e.g., the Flood, the calling of Abraham); and (3) *Christ and the New Testament must have interpretive priority over the Old Testament (OT).*[3] We must *"listen to Him"* (Matt. 17:5: Mark 9:7; Luke 9:35) (emphasis Maxcey's).[4]

Following Christotelic hermeneutics results in certain key tenets. Thus A. Blake White defines NCT as follows:[5]

1. One plan of God centered in Jesus Christ.

2. The Old Testament should be interpreted in light of the New Testament.

---

3   If you are interested in a Bible study utilizing those principles, check out: Heather A. Kendall, *God's Unfolding Story of Salvation: The Christ-Centered Biblical Storyline* (Eugene, OR: Resource Publications, 2012). Every lesson in the OT has this application: "The Old Testament points to Jesus through preparation for his birth, direct prophecy, pictures or types, and anticipation. Which of these apply in this lesson?"

4   Zachary Maxcey, cited by Gary D. Long, *New Covenant Theology: Time for a More Accurate Way,* 160, 161.

5   A. Blake White, *New Covenant Theology Questions Answered,* 1. Unpublished paper, n.d.

3. The Old Covenant was temporary by divine design.

4. The Law is a unit.[6]

5. Christians are not under the Law of Moses but the 'Law' of Christ.[7]

6. All members of the New Covenant community have the Holy Spirit.

7. The church is the eschatological Israel.[8]

In addition, Gary Long defines NCT in this way:

> NCT may be defined broadly as *God's eternal purpose progressively revealed in the commandments and promises of the biblical covenants of the OT and fulfilled in the New Covenant of Jesus Christ*. Its major themes may be summarily described with reference to:
>
> • *God's eternal purpose of redemption*: covenantly revealed and administered through biblical covenants beginning with a pre-fall covenant of obedience with Adam (Rom. 5:12–19; Eph. 2:12) and a post-fall covenant of promise (Gen. 3:15);[9]
>
> • *Hermeneutics*: consistent interpretation of the OT in light of the NT (Luke 24:27; II Cor. 1:20);

---

6   Meaning the Mosaic Law.

7   A. Blake White, *The Law of Christ: A Theological Proposal* (Frederick, MD: New Covenant Media, 2010). On page 83, he states, "I want to propose the following five points regarding the law of Christ: 1. The law of Christ is the law of love. 2. The law of Christ is Christ's example. 3. The law of Christ is the teaching of Christ. 4. The law of Christ is the teaching of Christ's apostles. 5. The law of Christ is the whole canon interpreted in light of Christ." Some have a tendency to ignore rule #5 leading to the error of Marcion (ignoring the Old Testament).

8   I think he means that the history of the nation of Israel culminates and finds its fulfillment in the church.

9   Some teach that the first covenant was a pre-fall covenant of obedience with Adam. Not everyone agrees since the Bible never uses the word covenant in reference to Adam.

- *The people of God*: all the elect of God throughout time first constituted as the church at Pentecost (Acts 1:4–5), but not before (John 7:39; 17:21–22; Col. 1:26–27; Heb. 11:39–40), as one corporate spiritual body in union with Christ (I Cor. 12:13; Eph. 2:19–21; Col. 1:18, 24); and

- *The law of God*: the two greatest commandments of God—love of God and neighbor (Matt. 22:36–40)—are innate law known instinctively by man (Rom. 2:14–15) created in God's image (Gen. 1:27). Upon these two greatest commandments all of God's covenantly written laws depend as administered under biblical covenants, which culminate in the New Covenant (NC) law of Christ (I Cor. 9:20–21; Romans 13:8–10; Galatians 6:2; Heb. 8:6, 13; James 2:8; I John 5:3). Innate law is righteous and unchanging. Covenantal law is written, righteous and changeable (Heb. 7:12) worked out in history in accordance with God's eternal purpose (Eph. 1:11; 3:11; II Tim. 1:9) (emphasis Long's).[10]

FINAL THOUGHTS

Since 1981, NCT has been a grass roots movement separating itself from Reformed Baptist theology. The covenant theologian Richard Barcellos complained that NCT was not a monolithic movement in his book, *In Defence of the Decalogue: A Critique of New Covenant Theology*.[11]

As far as I am concerned, not being monolithic is desirable. As we have seen, a well-developed creed easily results in allegiance to it over loyalty to the Bible itself. Presently there are several areas where there is either disagreement or fuzzy thinking: the existence of a pre-fall covenant with Adam, the place of the law in the life of the new covenant believer, what constitutes the law of Christ, the ministry of the Holy Spirit in the Old and

---

10 Gary D. Long, *New Covenant Theology: Time for a More Accurate Way*, 2, 3.
11 Richard Barcellos, *In Defence of the Decalogue*, preface.

New Testaments, the correct mode of baptism, church government, and eschatology.[12] I pray that these disagreements will not cause further divisions among new covenant theologians now or in the future.

Furthermore, may new covenant theologians never forget their roots—a belief in the doctrines of grace and the believers-only church. May the reader appreciate the courage of Jon Zens, John Reisinger, Ron McKinney and Gary Long for questioning the teaching of other believers. The history of NCT is not over; it will continue on into the future. Those four men are still actively promoting NCT. But, when John Reisinger officially passed the mantle on to a much younger generation, he ended an era.

May we continually be students of the Word like the saints at Berea—testing the Scriptures to see if what we hear others say is true (Acts 17:11). May no one glory or marvel except in the cross of Christ! May we worship King Jesus in unity of spirit!

---

12 Heather A. Kendall, *A Tale of Two Kingdoms* (Belleville, ON: Guardian, 2006). I outline the history of the Jewish people in the 400 years between the Old and New Testaments in Chapter 11, "The Silent Years." In that chapter I also trace the development of Jewish thought regarding God's kingdom which resulted in the idea of a millennium.

FURTHER GLIMPSES OF NEW COVENANT THEOLOGY DEVELOPING BEFORE THE REFORMATION

IGNATIUS, BISHOP OF ANTIOCH, MARTYRED C. AD 115

There is only one true God. For a time, God revealed himself through the prophets who lived under the laws of Judaism. But now God displays himself through Jesus Christ, God's Son.

To the Magnesians, vi – vii

Do not be led astray by strange doctrines and ancient unprofitable myths. For if we are still living according to Judaism to this day, then we are admitting that we have not received grace. For the divinely inspired prophets lived in expectation of Jesus Christ: and therefore they were persecuted, being inspired by his grace so that unbelievers might be convinced that there is one God who has displayed himself through Jesus Christ his

Son, who is his Word that proceeds from silence, who in all respects was pleasing to him who sent him.[1]

IRENAEUS, BISHOP OF LYONS, C AD 130–200

According to Henry Bettenson:

Irenaeus may justly be called the first biblical theologian; for him the Bible is not a collection of proof-texts as it is for the Apologists, but a continuous record of God's self-disclosure and his dealings with man, reaching its culmination in the person and work of Christ.[2]

Irenaeus understood the progressive way that God has worked throughout history to work out his plan of salvation.

Against Heresies, 4.14.2

So also God from the beginning fashioned man with a view to displaying his bounty. He chose the patriarchs with a view to their salvation; he prepared a people, teaching them, obstinate as they were to follow God; he set up prophets on earth, thus accustoming man to hear his Spirit and have fellowship with God. He indeed had need of none; but to those who had need of him he granted his fellowship; and for those who were pleasing to him he drafted a plan of salvation, like an architect; and to those who saw him not in Egypt he gave guidance; to those who were restless in the wilderness he gave the Law which meted their needs; to those who entered into the good land he presented a worthy inheritance; for those who return to the Father he kills the fatted calf and gives them the best robe; in many different ways he restores man to harmony and salvation. For this reason John says in the Apocalypse: "His voice was like the voice of many waters." The "many waters" represent the

---

1   Ignatius, "To the Magnesians," vi – vii, in *The Early Christian Fathers,* translated and edited by Henry Bettenson (New York, NY: Oxford University Press, 1956), 58.

2   Henry Bettenson, translator and editor, *The Early Christian Fathers* ((New York, NY: Oxford University Press, 1956), 17.

Spirit of God; and in truth they are many, because the Father is rich and great. Through all these waters the Word passed and gave assistance ungrudgingly to those who submitted to him, prescribing laws suitable for every condition.[3]

Irenaeus also taught that Abraham is the father of all believers whether born circumcised, like the Israelites, or uncircumcised, like the Gentiles. God unites them through Christ into one building, the church. Moreover the law of works, or the Mosaic Covenant, was temporary.

Against Heresies, 4.25.1

For thus it had behoved the sons of Abraham [to be], whom God has raised up to him from the stones, and caused to take a place beside him who was made the chief and the forerunner of our faith (who did also receive the covenant of circumcision, after that justification by faith which had pertained to him, when he was yet in uncircumcision, so that in him both covenants might be prefigured, that he might be the father of all who follow the Word of God, and who sustain a life of pilgrimage in this world, that is, of those who from among the circumcision and of those from among the uncircumcision are faithful, even as also "Christ is the chief corner-stone" sustaining all things); and He gathered into the one faith of Abraham those who, from either covenant, are eligible for God's building. But this faith which is in uncircumcision, as connecting the end with the beginning, has been made [both] the first and the last. For, as I have shown, it existed in Abraham antecedently to circumcision, as it also did in the rest of the righteous who pleased God: and in these last times, it again sprang up among mankind through the coming of the Lord. But circumcision and the law of works occupied the intervening period.[4]

---

3   Irenaeus, "Against Heresies," 4.14.2, in *The Early Christian Fathers*, translated and edited by Henry Bettenson (New York, NY: Oxford University Press, 1956), 91, 92.

4   Irenaeus, *Against Heresies*, 4.25.1, last modified (date) accessed January 7, 2015, http://www.earlychristianwritings.com/text/irenaeus-book4.html.

ORIGEN, C AD 185–254

God has chosen all who will be saved from the beginning of the world to the end. Origen included all believers in the church no matter when they were born. His idea of the church is different from covenant theology, however, which allows for a visible mixed-multitude of believers and non-believers. Origen does not appear to be writing about the visible church of Christ established after Pentecost; rather the sum total of all the elect for whom Christ died.

Comm. In Canticum Canticorum ii

I would not have you suppose that the "bride of Christ" or the Church is spoken of only after the coming of the Saviour in the flesh: but rather from the beginning of the human race, from the very foundation of the world; nay, I may follow Paul in tracing the origin of this mystery even further, before the foundation of the world. For Paul says: "He chose us in Christ before the foundation of the world, that we should be holy..." (Eph 1: 4, 5). The Apostle also says that the Church is built on the foundation not only of the Apostles but also of prophets. (Eph 2:20). Now Adam is numbered among the prophets, and he prophesied the "great mystery in respect of Christ and the Church" when he said: "For this reason a man shall leave his father and his mother and shall cleave to his wife, and the two shall be in one flesh" (Gen 2:24). For the Apostle is clearly speaking of these when he says: "This mystery is great; but I am speaking in respect of Christ and the Church" (Eph 5:32). Further the Apostle also says: "For he so loved the Church that he gave himself for her, sanctifying her with the washing of water" (Eph 5: 25, 26). And in this he shows that it is not the case that she did not exist before. For how could he love her if she did not exist? Without doubt she existed and so he loved her, for the Church existed in all the saints who had been from the beginning of time. Thus, loving the Church, he came to her. And as his "children share in flesh and blood, so he also was made partaker of these" (Heb 2:14) and gave himself for them. For these saints were the Church, which he loved so as to increase it in numbers, to improve it with virtues, and by the "charity of perfection" (cf. Col 3:14) transfer it from earth to heaven.[5]

AUGUSTINE, AD 354–430

Augustine taught that Jesus deserves greater honor than Moses. God kept his land promise to Abraham's seed through the Israelites while he kept his promise of blessing to all the nations through Christ.

The City of God, Book 16, Chapter XLIII

Moses being dead, Joshua ruled the people and led them into the land of promise, dividing it amongst them. And by these two glorious captains were strange battles won, and they were ended with happy success; God himself avouching that the losers' sins and not the winners' merits were the causes of those conquests. After these two, the land of promise were ruled by judges, that Abraham's seed might see the first promise fulfilled, concerning the land of Canaan, though not as yet concerning the nations of all the earth, for that was to be fulfilled by the coming of Christ in the flesh, and the faith of the gospel, not the precepts of the law, which was insinuated in this, that it was not Moses, who received the law, but Joshua, whose name God also changed, that led the people into the promised land.[6]

Tom Wells mentions another quote of Augustine: "Now there are many things called God's covenants besides *those two great ones, the old and the new,* which any one who pleases may read

---

5   Origen, "Comm. In Canticum Canticorum," *ii,* in *The Early Christian Fathers,* translated and edited by Henry Bettenson (New York, NY: Oxford University Press, 1956), 338, 339.

6   Augustine, *Saint Augustine: The City of God,* vol. 2, edited by R.V.G. Tasker (New York, NY: E. P. Dutton, 1962), 142.

and know" (italics Wells').[7] In this quote Augustine recognized two main covenants, the old and the new—implying important distinctions between them.

THOMAS AQUINAS, C. AD 1227–1274

Aquinas uses the terms old law and new law to mean old covenant and new covenant. Thus he teaches that the new covenant is superior to the old. This implies that the old covenant has passed away and the new covenant has replaced it.

Summa Theologica

> [I]t was fitting that the perfect law of the New Testament should be given immediately [i.e. by God himself]; but that the Old Law should be given to men by the ministers of God, *i.e.*, by the angels. It is thus that the Apostle at the beginning of his epistle to the *Hebrews* (i.2) proved the excellence of the New Law over the Old; because in the New Testament *God hath spoken to us by His Son*, whereas in the Old Testament the word was *spoken by angels* (ii.2) (italics Wells').[8]

As Wells explains,

> Terminology changes with the passage of centuries. When we come to the medieval period we find frequent reference to the *Old* and *New Law* rather than Old and New Covenants, and that continued in the Roman Catholic Church into this century (italics Wells').[9]

---

7 Augustine, *The City of God*, 16.27, last modified (date) accessed October 23, 2015, http://www.newadvent.org/fathers/120116.htm ; cited by Tom Wells, "The Christian Appeal of a New Covenant Theology," in *New Covenant Theology*, 25.

8 Thomas Aquinas, *Summa Theologica*, first part of the second part, 13, ques. 98, art. 3, last modified (date), accessed October 23, 2015, http://www.newadvent.org/summa/2098.htm; cited by Tom Wells, "The Christian Appeal of a New Covenant Theology," in *New Covenant Theology*, 26.

9 Tom Wells, "The Christian Appeal of a New Covenant Theology," in *New Covenant Theology*, 26.

BIBLIOGRAPHY

- Aquinas, Thomas. *Summa Theologica*. First Part of the Second Part. Question 98 Article 3. Last Modified (Date). Accessed October 23, 2015. http://www.newadvent.org/summa/2098.htm.

- Augustine. *An Augustine Synthesis*. Arranged by Erich Przywara. New York, NY: Harper & Brothers, 1958.

- Augustine. *Saint Augustine: The City of God*. Vol. 2. Edited by R.V.G. Tasker. New York, NY: E. P. Dutton, 1962.

- Augustine. *The City of God*. 16.27. Last Modified (Date). Accessed October 23, 2015. http://www.newadvent.org/fathers/120116.htm.

- Barnabas of Alexandria. *Epistle of Barnabas*. Chapter 2. Last Modified (Date). Accessed September 26, 2014. http://earlychristianwritings.com/text/barnabas-roberts.html.

- Bettenson, Henry. Editor and translator. *The Early Christian Fathers*. New York, NY: Oxford University Press, 1956.

- Bresson, Chad. "The Exceeding Righteousness of the New Covenant." Last Modified (June 2009). Accessed January 19, 2015. http://www.christourcovenant.blogspot.ca/2009/06/exceeding-righteousness-of-new-covenant.html.

- Bresson, Chad. "What Is New Covenant Theology?". Last Modified (November 2010). Accessed January 19, 2015. http://breusswane.blogspot.ca/2010/11/what-is-new-covenant-theology.html.

- Bresson, Chad. "What Is New Covenant Theology?". Last Modified (May 2011). Accessed January 19, 2015. http://breusswane.blogspot.ca/2011/05/what-is-new-covenant-theology.html.

- Bresson, Chad. "The Incarnation of the Abstract: New Covenant Theology and the Enfleshment of the Law," 2, 3. Last Modified (2011). Accessed January 19, 2015. http://www.ncbf.us/thinktank2011/TheIncarnationoftheAbstract-NCTThinkTank2011.pdf.

- Bunyan, John. *Of the Law and the Christian.* Last Modified (Date). Accessed January 7, 2015. http://solochristo.com/theology/nct/JohnBunyan_LawandtheChristian.html.

- Chantry, Thomas and David Dykstra. *Holding Communion Together, The Reformed Baptists: The First Fifty Years, Divided & United.* Birmingham, AL: Solid Ground Christian Books, 2014.

- Chantry, Walter J. "Building a New Work." Last Modified (Date). Accessed March 25, 2014. http://www.gracebaptistcarlisle.org/e_reisinger_bio.htm.

- Chantry, Walter J. Personal letter to Jon Zens. "Law and Ministry in the Church." *Searching Together,* 40, no. 01–04, 40th Anniversary (2014): 23.

- Christman, Ted. "A Letter From A Concerned Church Leader To Jon Zens (1979)." *Searching Together,* 40, no. 01–04, 40th Anniversary (2014): 55, 56.

- Chrysostom, John. *Commentary on Galatians 3.* Last Modified (Date). Accessed May 28, 2014. http://sacred-texts.com/chr/ecf/113/1130008/htm.

- Coad, F. Roy. *History of the Brethren Movement.* Grand Rapids, MI: Eerdmans, 1968.

- Crisp, Tobias. "Christian Liberty No Licentious Doctrine." Last Modified (Date). Accessed March 30, 2015. http://www.pbministries.org/Theology/Crisp,Tobias/sermon8.htm.

- Dollar, George W. *A History of Fundamentalism in America.* Greenville, SC: Bob Jones University Press, 1973.

- Estep, William R. *The Anabaptist Story.* Rev. ed. Grand Rapids, MI: Eerdmans, 1975.

- Fay, Roger. "Rolfe Barnard (1904–1969)," 1. Last Modified (Date). Accessed January 8, 2015. www.reformation-today.org/articles/Rolfe_Barnard_(1904–1969).pdf.

- Fellows, Roger. "Bill Payne and the Sovereign Grace Movement in Canada." 1–4, 6, 7, 14. Unpublished paper, n.d.

- Fellows, Roger. "The Law and The Christian." 6. Unpublished pamphlet, March 26, 2002.

- *The First London Confession of Faith.* 1646 ed. Belton, TX: Sovereign Grace Ministries, 2004.

- Frey, René. Ed. *SEMBEQ: 40 Years: Celebrating the Faithfulness of God.* Montreal, QC: SEMBEQ, n.d.

- Garlington, Don. [Letter to the editor]. *Baptist Reformation Review,* 7, no. 4 (Winter 1978): 17–19.

- Gentry, Peter J. and Stephen J. Wellum. *Kingdom through Covenant: A Biblical-Theological Understanding of the Covenants.* Wheaton, IL: Crossway, 2012.

- George, Gary. *Hermeneutical Flaws of Dispensationalism.* Frederick, MD: New Covenant Media, 2012.

- Gilliland, J. David. "The New Heart, The New Covenant, and Not So New Controversies: A Critique of the Modern 'Grace Movement.'" Part 1 of 3. *Sound of Grace,* no. 197 (May 2013): 7, 13, 18.

- Gilliland, J. David. "The New Heart, The New Covenant, and Not So New Controversies: A Critique of the Modern 'Grace Movement.'" Part 2 of 3. *Sound of Grace,* no. 198 (June 2013): 12, 18.

- Gilliland, J. David. "The New Heart, The New Covenant, and Not So New Controversies: A Critique of the Modern 'Grace Movement.'" Part 3 of 3. *Sound of Grace*, no. 199 (July-August 2013): 19.

- "God's Covenant." In *The Baptist Confession of Faith (1689)*. Article 7 No. 3. Revised by C. H. Spurgeon. Last Modified (Date). Accessed February 23, 2008. http://www.spurgeon. org//~phil/creeds/bcof.htm.

- Goodin, Douglas. "An Important Announcement." *Sound of Grace*, no. 211 (October 2014): 14, 15.

- Hamilton Jr., James M. *God's Glory in Salvation through Judgment: A Biblical Theology.* Wheaton, IL: Crossway, 2010.

- Hoch, Jr., Carl B. *All Things New: The Significance of Newness for Biblical Theology.* Grand Rapids, MI: Baker Books, 1995.

- Hulse, Erroll. *An Introduction to the Baptists.* 2nd ed. Haywards Heath, England: Carey, 1976.

- Huntington, William. Last Modified (Date). Accessed March 26, 2015. http://users.rcn.com/delong/williamh.html.

- Ignatius. "To the Magnesians," vi – vii. In *The Early Christian Fathers.* Translated and edited by Henry Bettenson. New York, NY: Oxford University Press, 1956.

- Irenaeus. *Against Heresies,* 4.9.1. Last Modified (Date). Accessed January 7, 2015. http://www.earlychristianwritings.com/text/ irenaeus-book4.html.

- Irenaeus. "Against Heresies," 4.14.2. In *The Early Christian Fathers.* Translated and edited by Henry Bettenson. New York, NY: Oxford University Press, 1956

- Irenaeus. *Against Heresies,* 4.25.1. Last Modified (Date). Accessed January 7, 2015. http://www.earlychristianwritings.com/text/ irenaeus-book4.html.

- Johnson, Phil. "Here's a real gold mine." Last Modified (Date). Accessed January 22, 2015. http://teampyro.blogspot.ca/2006/03/heres-real-gold-mine.html.

- Kendall, Heather A. "The Bible's Storyline: How It Affects the Doctrine of Salvation." *Journal for Baptist Theology & Ministry*, 8. no. 1 (Spring 2011): 62, 64. Last Modified (Spring 2011). Accessed January 28, 2015. http://baptistcenter.net/journals/JBTM_8-1_Spring_2011.pdf#page=62.

- Kendall, Heather A. *God's Unfolding Story of Salvation: The Christ-Centered Biblical Storyline*. Eugene, OR: Resource Publications, 2012.

- "The Law of God." In *The Baptist Confession of Faith (1689)*. Article 19 No. 1, 2, 7, 9. Revised by C. H. Spurgeon. Last Modified (Date). Accessed February 23, 2008. http://www.spurgeon.org//~phil/creeds/bcof.htm.

- Lee, Francis Nigel. [Letter to the editor]. *Baptist Reformation Review*, 11, no. 1 (Spring 1982): 19, 20.

- Long, Gary D. "The Christian Sabbath—Lord's Day Controversy," 2, 3: footnote 3, 23, 24. Last Modified (Date). Accessed January 29, 2015. http://www.ptsco.org/The Christian Sabbath booklet.pdf.

- Long, Gary D. *Context! Evangelical Views On The Millennium Examined*. 3rd ed. Charleston, SC: www.CreateSpace.com, 2011.

- Long, Gary D. "New Covenant Theology: What It Is and How It Differs from Covenant Theology," 15, 16. Last Modified (Date). Accessed November 2, 2015. http://gospelpedlar.com/articles/Bible/n_c_theology/NCT-What-It.pdf.

- Long, Gary D. "New Covenant Theology," 1. Last Modified (2013). Accessed November 2, 2015. http://www.ptsco.org/NCT Brochoure Text 2013.pdf.

- Long, Gary D. *New Covenant Theology: Time for a More Accurate Way*. Charleston, SC: www.CreateSpace.com, 2013.

- Long, Gary D. *Biblical Law and Ethics: Absolute and Covenantal.* Charleston, SC: www.Create Space.com, 2014.

- Lucas, Richard. "Are you Reformed? (Part 2)." Last Modified (Date). Accessed March 13, 2014. http://www.credomag. com/2012/07/27/are-you-reformed-part-2/.

- Martin, Steve. "A Brief History of Reformed Baptists." Last Modified (Date). Accessed March 16, 2014. http://www.reformedbaptist.org/ who-we-are/a-brief-history-of-reformed-baptists.

- Martyr, Justin. *Dialogue with Trypho.* Chapter 11. Last Modified (Date). Accessed March 24, 2014. http://www.bombaxo.com/ trypho.html.

- Mason, William. *The Believer's Pocket Companion: The One Thing needful To Make Poor Sinners Rich & Miserable Sinners Happy.* First pub. 1773. Willow Street, PA: Old Paths Publications, 2000.

- Maxcey, Zachary S. "Picture-Fufillment New Covenant Theology: A Positive Theological Development?", 3. Last Modified (Date). Accessed November 2, 2015. http://www.ptsco. org/Picture-Fulfillment%20NCT.pdf.

- Maxcey, Zachary S. "Historical Forerunners of New Covenant Theology." Part 1 of 3. *Providence Theological Seminary Journal,* no. 1 (Nov 2014): 6.

- Maxcey, Zachary S. "Historical Forerunners of New Covenant Theology." Part 2 of 3. *Providence Theological Seminary Journal,* no. 2 (February 2014): 14, 15.

- Maxcey, Zachary S. "Historical Forerunners of New Covenant Theology." Part 3 of 3. *Providence Theological Seminary Journal,* no. 3 (May 2015): 8.

- McCulley, Mark. *Studies in History and Ethics.* Malin, OR: BREM, 1982.

- McKinney, Ronald W. "Adoption: The Crowning Blessing of The New Covenant," 1, 4, 12, 13. Unpublished paper. n.d.

- Meyer, Jason C. *The End of the Law: Mosaic Covenant in Pauline Theology*. Nashville, TN: B&H Academic, 2009.

- Nettles, Tom. "The Rise & Demise of Calvinism Among Southern Baptists." *Founders Journal*, 2. Last Modified (Date). Accessed January 25, 2014. http://www.founders.org/journal/fj19/article1. html.

- *The New Lexicon Webster's Dictionary of the English Language*. Canadian Edition. New York, NY: Lexicon, 1988.

- Origen. "Comm. In Canticum Canticorum," *ii*. In *The Early Christian Fathers*. Translated and edited by Henry Bettenson. New York, NY: Oxford University Press, 1956.

- Origen. *Contra Celsum*, 8.5. Last Modified (Date). Accessed May 28, 2014. http://www.gnosis.org/library/orig_cc8.htm.

- Orr, James. *The History and Literature of The Early Church*. London: Hodder and Stoughton, 1913.

- Reisinger, John G. "When Should a Christian Leave a Church?". Last Modified (Date). Accessed March 31, 2014. http:// solochristo.com/theology/Church/reiwh.htm.

- Reisinger, John G. *The Law/Grace Controversy: A Defense of the Sword & Trowel and the Council on Baptist Theology*. Berryville, VA: Grace Abounding Ministries, 1982.

- Reisinger, John G. *Abraham's Four Seeds*. Frederick, MD: New Covenant Media, 1998.

- Reisinger, John G. "An Open Letter to Dr. R. C. Sproul." Last Modified (Date). Accessed August 28, 2013. http://solochristo. com/theology/nct/reisinger-lettertosproul.htm.

- Reisinger, John G. *Tablets of Stone & The History of Redemption*. Frederick, MD: New Covenant Media, 2004.

- Reisinger, John G. *Continuity and Discontinuity*. Frederick, MD: New Covenant Media, 2011.

- Reisinger, John G. *New Covenant Theology & Prophecy*. Frederick, MD: New Covenant Media, 2012.

- Reisinger, John G. "A Critique of the New View of NCT." *Sound of Grace,* no. 185 (March 2012): 2.

- Reisinger, John G. "John Reisinger on the 200th Issue of Sound of Grace." *Sound of Grace,* no. 200 (September 2013): 2.

- Reisinger, John G. "An Important Announcement." *Sound of Grace,* no. 211 (October 2014): 14.

- Rishel, Joel. "The Impact of A. W. Pink." Last Modified (Date). Accessed March 26, 2014. http://www.biblebaptistelmont.org/ BBC/library/pink.html.

- Scalyer, Lloyd Elias. "It was there all the time....", 1. Unpublished pamphlet, n.d.

- Schreiner, Thomas R. *The King in His Beauty: A Biblical Theology of the Old and New Testaments*. Ada, MI: Baker Academic, 2013.

- Sitton, David. *Reckless Abandon*. Greenville, SC: Ambassador International, 2011.

- Sproul, R. C. *What is Reformed Theology?: Understanding the Basics*. Grand Rapids, MI: Baker Books, 1997.

- Stewart, Kenneth J. "The Points of Calvinism: Retrospect and Prospect," 189, 190. Last Modified (Date). Accessed March 13, 2014. http://responsivereiding.files.wordpress.com/2009/03/ points-of-calvinism-retrospect-and-prospect1.pdf.

- Swanson, Dennis M. "Introduction to New Covenant Theology," 152, 153. Last Modified (Date). Accessed March 25, 2015. http://www.tms.edu/tmsj/tmsj18f.pdf.

- Walker, Williston. *A History of the Christian Church*. 3rd edition. Revised by Robert T. Handy. New York, NY: Charles Scribner's, 1970.

- Wells, Tom and Fred Zaspel. *New Covenant Theology*. Frederick, MD: New Covenant Media, 2002.

- Wells, Tom. *The Priority of Jesus Christ*. Frederick, MD: New Covenant Media, 2005.

- White, A. Blake. *The Newness of the New Covenant*. Frederick, MD: New Covenant Media, 2008.

- White, A. Blake. *The Law of Christ: A Theological Proposal*. Frederick, MD: New Covenant Media, 2010.

- White, A. Blake. "New Covenant Theology Questions Answered," 1. Unpublished paper, n.d.

- Zaspel, Fred G. "Why Do We Sin? Thoughts from James on Sovereignty, Sin, and Grace." In *Ministry of Grace: Essays in Honor of John G. Reisinger*. Edited by Steve West. 171. Frederick, MD: New Covenant Media, 2007.

- Zaspel, Fred G. *The New Covenant and New Covenant Theology*. Frederick, MD: New Covenant Media, 2011.

- Zens, Jon. "Is There A 'Covenant Of Grace?' ". *Baptist Reformation Review*, 6, no. 3 (Autumn 1977): 43, 51–53.

- Zens, Jon. "Crucial Thoughts On "Law" In The New Covenant." *Baptist Reformation Review*, 7, no. 3 (Spring 1978): 10, 14, 16, 17.

- Zens, Jon. "'This Is My Beloved Son…Hear Him': A Study Of The Development Of Law In The History Of Redemption." *Baptist Reformation Review*, 7, no. 4 (Winter 1978): 15, 26, 27, 34.

- Zens, Jon. "A Review Article of Walter Chantry's *God's Righteous Kingdom: The Law's Connection with the Gospel*." Last Modified (Date). Accessed March 31, 2014. http://solochristo.com/theology/nct/zens-chantry.htm.

- Zens, Jon. "After Ten Years: Observations and Burdens On My Heart." *Baptist Reformation Review*, 11, no. 1, (Spring 1982): 24.

- Zens, Jon. "A More Gradual Journey Out of the Pastorate." Last Modified (Date). Accessed March 21, 2014. http://www.housechurchresource.org/expastors/gradual-zens.html.

- Zens, Jon. "Law and Ministry in the Church: An Informal Essay On Some Historical Developments (1972–1984)." *Searching Together*, 40, no. 01–04, 40th Anniversary (2014): 17, 21, 22, 24, 27, 28, 31, 32.

- Zens, Jon. "A Letter From A Concerned Church Leader To Jon Zens (1979)." *Searching Together*, 40, no. 01–04, 40th Anniversary (2014): 56–59, 61.

For more information about Heather Kendall
or to contact her for speaking engagements,
please visit *www.tale2k.com*

Many voices. One message.

Quoir is a boutique publishing company
with a single message: Christ is all.
Our books explore both His
cosmic nature and corporate expression.

For more information, please visit
www.quoir.com

CPSIA information can be obtained
at www.ICGtesting.com
Printed in the USA
BVOW08s0849050218
507254BV00027B/1175/P